Escaping the
Family
Time
Trap

A Practical Guide
for Overbusy Families

Barbara DeGrote-Sorensen

David Allen Sorensen

Augsburg
MINNEAPOLIS

ESCAPING THE FAMILY TIME TRAP
A Practical Guide for Overbusy Families

Scripture passages are from the Revised Standard Version of the Bible, copyright © 1946, 1952, 1971, 1989 by the Division of Christian Education of the National Council of the Churches of Christ in the USA. Used by permission.

Material from *Stress and the Healthy Family* by Dolores Curran is copyright © Dolores Curran and used by permission.

Material from *Traits of a Healthy Family* by Dolores Curran is copyright © Dolores Curran and used by permission.

Material from "Lies Parents Tell Themselves about Why They Work," *U.S. News and World Report,* is copyright © May 12, 1997, *U.S. News and World Report* and used by permission. Visit their Web site at <www.usnews.com> for additional information.

Cover image copyright © 2001 Tony Stone Images. Used by permission.
Cover design by David Meyer
Book design by Michelle L. Norstad and Timothy W. Larson

Library of Congress Cataloging-in-Publication Data

DeGrote-Sorensen, Barbara, –
Escaping the family time trap: a practical guide for overbusy families /
Barbara DeGrote-Sorensen, David Sorensen.
   p. cm.
Includes bibliographical references.
ISBN 0-8066-3813-3 (alk. paper)
1. Family—Time management. I. Sorensen, David Allen, – II. Title.

HQ734.D428 2001
640'.43'085—dc21   2001022085

The paper used in this publication meets the minimum requirements of American National Standard for Information Sciences—Permanence of Paper for Printed Library Materials, ANSI Z329.48-1984. ♾ ™

Manufactured in the U.S.A.   AF 9-3813

05   04   03   02   01   1   2   3   4   5   6   7   8   9   10

Contents

Introduction

Create a Right Spirit

Over the past few years, we have talked to hundreds of parents in various stages of life and studied material on family, stress, time management, and lifestyle. We were not surprised to find that although many of the people we talked with understood the rigors of time management, the majority still lamented a loss of family together time.

We all know more than we want to know about organizing calendars and conquering the paper chase. We know how to de-stress, de-clutter, and the consequences of sleep deprivation. We've learned how to use technology to help speed up some of the daily grind, and we have dutifully prioritized our daily planners, or at least thought about doing so. In spite of our best intentions to make time fit into twenty-four-hour segments, we still often feel that we are shortchanging ourselves or those most important to us. These are the moments when we bang our heads on the table and fantasize about grabbing everyone at home and escaping it all.

What Do We Really Want as a Family?

We want to connect, build relationships, and be content in one another's company. We want to eat supper together, laugh more, and do less without feeling guilty about it. Do I hear another head going down? The best thing about head banging is that it feels so good when you stop.

1

And a lot of people have stopped. According to a 1995 issue of *U.S. News and World Report*, 48 percent of Americans say that over the preceding five years they made decisions that could simplify their lives.[1] When asked to choose between more money or more free time, 51 percent chose more free time. Many who have their hands on the pulse of American culture are asking, "Are we changing from a work-orientated to a relationship-orientated society?"[2] The answer is coming back a tentative yes.

In Part I of this book, we will identify characteristics of your family, what your family considers important, how you connect with each other, and what you're longing for. A survey in chapter 2 and some open-ended questions will augment your own gut feelings about these things.

What's Stopping Us from Connecting?

That more of us are seeking to connect is good news for families. But it's been a long time since we've been given permission not to work so hard and want so much. Sometimes it's hard to connect because we can't remember who we really are as a family. Some of us have old habits to break. Others of us need to do some personal reflecting so we can be honest with ourselves and those whose lives we share. We need to build new time-saving routines into our daily activities and get downright nasty about things that steal time away from our first priorities.

In Part II, we will look at some of these time burglars and the difficulties work and our many activities present to our families.

How Can We Create Connectedness?

The first steps are the simplest. A book dealing with family time traps could easily settle for focusing merely on changing behavior. But merely making changes in one's behavior addresses only the symptoms. As Albert Einstein once said,

"A problem cannot be solved with the same type of thinking that created it."[3] Because it was our thinking, our own choices, that got us disconnected in the first place, we will need first to change our thinking in order to retie the knot.

First, create a right spirit. Talk with the Good Shepherd, the one who knows a lot about getting sheep back into the fold, connecting up lost sons with fathers, returning a "dead one" to his sisters, assuring a worried father that his daughter will be well. Jesus cares about families and their relationships with one another. He cares about your family, too.

Expect that conversation to continue on a daily basis. Escaping the family time trap is not a one-time event but an ongoing process of confession and forgiveness, resurrection days, Good Fridays, small steps, giant leaps of faith, and a whole lot of grace backing up our good intentions. It's worth the effort. Like any good process, the joy is in the journey.

Part III of this book will help you move from longings to practical realities. You will have a chance to reclaim family rituals, reconnect in some new ways, and perhaps even redefine family to include others as we demonstrate to our children the importance of connecting with one's extended family and serving the world at large.

What this book will not give you is a definitive list of criteria for a time-friendly family or a one-size-fits-all answer. Rather, through reflection and hands-on activities, we hope you can uncover for yourself what works for you, your own family-customized answer to the family time trap.

* * * * *

On a personal note, this book has taken its own long journey toward publication. Like many, we've been responding altogether too much to the tyranny of the urgent: we drop some important things to attend to whatever seems to be at hand. So about five years elapsed since we first began writing articles and book proposals. We just didn't have time to write the book. More than we'd like, we apportioned our time based on what came at us with the most energy and immediacy rather than on what we really found important. On the other hand, with three teenagers at home, there's been plenty of urgent "stuff" going on that perhaps rightly relegated this book to a backseat. Suffice it to say that we've written these words from the front lines. No ivory-tower lifestyle philosophies here. The five-year wait is a necessary process of ideas cooking in some of life's juices.

So, let us begin. Let us ask the Lord to bless our journey and create a right spirit in our hearts and in our homes. Let us give thanks for those we call our own. Let us begin to take those first steps toward reclaiming our family relationships and giving them their rightful place in our priorities. We pray that the Holy Spirit will guide and bless you in this endeavor.

How to Use This Book

This is a hands-on book. It's intended for you and your children. Early in the book, you and your family will be given an opportunity to take a personal survey to help assess your time needs and restraints as they relate to your family. The sections in each chapter are intended to give you some insight and information from which to adapt the discussion prompts and family-based activities, called "Connecting Points," to your family's needs. How you use these discussion starters and connecting points will depend on the age of your children and just how far you want to go with the ideas.

Consider keeping a scrapbook of your family adventure. Appoint a photographer (rotate this job on occasion if you want everyone's face in the book), someone to paste in the pictures, and someone else to write down quotes from the day. Start a family journal and pass it around to get responses from the discussion prompts. There are no expectations here—no required assignments. You aren't being graded on your performance. This should be fun, not work.

This is opportunity time—a time to enjoy one another and be blessed by the gift of family as God intended.

Although the activities are designed for individual families, there is a benefit to sharing the planning with others in a small group. Used as a small-group study (see the small-group Study Guide at the end of the book), *Escaping the Family Time Trap* allows parents to share what's working for them as well as to find support when things are rocky. Consider asking a couple or two whose children are grown to act as mentors for your group. Start the study off with an all-family picnic, potluck, or kid-friendly supper that includes all participating families. Kids love to be with other kids, and you won't feel that you're leaving your family one more night to go and study about how to find more family time. Consider sharing a baby-sitter for the evening so the parents can meet, share stories, and make plans for future activities. To start the evening, plan one fun game that can be enjoyed by all. Later, as you progress through the chapters, consider searching out a ministry need outside your own group, a person or place where your family or study group can expand the definition of *family* to include those outside your own circle (see chapter 9).

However you choose to use this book, we hope that you will find the balance between study, reflection, discussion, and activity a benefit to you and all who share the process with you.

Part I

What Do We Really Want as a Family?

Chapter 1

Connectedness

We had run our Macintosh computer trouble-free for a few years before starting to get a handful of recurring troubles, annoying glitches, and full-blown crashes. At the recommendation of a friend, we purchased Norton Disk Doctor. One little disk that promised to clear up all our problems.

The Disk Doctor took a long time reading the degree of damage that had occurred on our hard drive through three years of inattention. Finally, it announced the verdict: severe fragmentation. That's what the computer said. Not slight fragmentation. Not moderate fragmentation. Not even serious fragmentation. Severe fragmentation! We sighed. The story of our lives.

Over the course of raising three children, we have encountered what we term "family fragmentation" on more than one occasion. Family fragmentation can creep up on the best of families. Inattentiveness, overscheduling, screwed-up priorities, and daily demands of caretakers all contribute to that feeling that we've misplaced something. Gaps appear in our conversations. Relationships lose their focus. We feel detached from one another, disengaged from the ones we cherish the most. We long for time to pull the pieces back together, reassemble the troops, and march into the day with linked arms and laughing voices. In reality, we'd settle for a sit-down supper and a night free of commitments. Families, like computers, take care. A little tune-up now and then may help prevent a full-blown crash later on.

Emphasis on family—the need to connect in a meaningful way to those who are important to us—is a natural extension of the simplicity trend that helped define the 1990s. Since then, the word *simplify* has come to appear on everything from cars to hair remover. When simplicity became a marketing trend, it was time to look for a new edge. What people wanted from simplicity, when all was said and done, wasn't less but more. More time to devote to the things in life that really matter. Simplicity wasn't just about less stuff. It was about connecting with ourselves and with others and, ultimately, with God.

So . . . what is the edge? What are people longing for today? Over and over, as we talked with families, we heard the word *connectedness.* What does it mean to connect? The dictionary uses words such as *relationship, bond, join,* and *union.* Families want to do more than share a roof. They want to enjoy each other, be there for one another, be companions, comrades. They want to create memories and traditions. They want to build a support system that will carry them through life. They want to establish a family identity.

Who are we as a family? What really matters to us? What does it mean to be a part of this family? During conversations based on these three simple family-identity questions, families like your own have shared with us about their attempts to be all they can be but find themselves lacking the time to be it. The following scenarios are just three composites of many that could be written from those conversations: Families that need more than just a time-management seminar. Families that need time to think through where they are going, what they want out of their time together, and what they would be willing to give up in order to get it. Families that were willing to work at connecting as a family.

Family Stories

Lois leaves for work at 3:30 P.M., about the time her kids get on the bus after school and head for home. She returns around nine o'clock, just in time to check in on the day's events before going to bed. The kids are old enough to get their own supper, and the oldest takes his schoolwork seriously. The middle boy would rather be in the woods and spends his off-school hours outside recovering from the effects of a day in the classroom. The younger girl waits for mom to come home. Roger, the husband, works out of town, comes home for a few days, and then leaves again for a few weeks. Family life revolves around these short visits. There is a sad tiredness in Lois's face. She doesn't want to move closer to Roger's workplace because of the disruption it would cause for the kids. She will maintain the home front, stay put, and create family as best she can.

* * * * *

It starts with showers. Carol gets up first mainly to get some quiet time to herself before breakfast, demands for lunch money, and rides after school begin. Her husband, Kenneth, pulls store-bought pancakes from the freezer and zaps them in the microwave while Carol gathers juice, plates, and silverware and heads toward the table. The family eats breakfast together. That is new this year—a small change in the morning schedule that helps them have time to discuss plans for the day. It only lasts five to seven minutes, but it's better than the breakfast-bar-in-hand departures that marked last year's morning take-off. They will return at different times as the day ends to touch base. Supper is laid out on the counter or kept warm in the oven, or there will be money and a note that reads "Buy Pizza" pinned on the kitchen bulletin board. It's a rare evening when everyone is home. With sports schedules, church commitments, and community obligations, evenings bring no relief to the go-go lifestyle. Carol counts heads at night to make sure everyone is home in bed, then shuts off the lights.

* * * * *

"The trouble is that this is a hurry-up society and kids don't hurry," Jana laments, trying to get her eleven-month-old's left leg into the snowsuit. "It's not enough to get myself to work on time; I have a whole life to live before I even step foot in that office." Jana and her husband, Jon, have thought about trying to make it with one job. But decisions they made before Meghan was born have them committed to a certain salary level. Jon has recently been offered a promotion in his practice, but it would mean longer work hours and more home responsibilities placed on Jana. On top of that, the in-laws keep complaining that they never get to see the baby. The family hasn't been to church in a month. The last time they attended worship, Jon spent most of the time walking the baby in the hall. "We're responsible for all this," Jana says. "We created our lives just the way we wanted them. How can we say we don't like it? What can we do to stop?"

What Do You Really Want for Your Family?

Barbara's mother has often recited the mantra "visualize, prayerize, and actualize" when embarking on a new adventure. It's good advice. Stop now and visualize your family the way you would like it to be. What would a normal day look and feel like? Where would you live? How would you live? How would you relate to one another? Imagine your family ten years into the future. Pray now for guidance as you start to take the steps needed to bring about your vision.

This book is a chance to slow the clock and direct your attention to those you've been given the opportunity to love. Creating family connections—that's what this book is about.

Connecting Points

• Ask your family members the three family-identity questions on page 10, or open up a discussion in your study group based on the three questions. Listen to one another's stories.

• Is your family reflected in any of the scenarios presented in this chapter? How are you different?

• If you could, what is one thing you would change about your family? What do you really want for your family? What would it take to make it happen?

• Intentionally slow the pace today: slow your driving, your steps as you go to answer the phone, your meal preparation, even your speech. Watch the effect of a slower pace on those around you. Let others in your family in on your secret and make a game out of it. Who can be the last one to the table for dinner or the last one into the car or the last one to brush their teeth?

• Here's a fun way to get connected fast. Gather your family or group into a circle. Pass a ball of yarn around one person's waist and then throw it to another person, who does the same thing. Continue the game until you've created a giant spider web. Now try to walk to the kitchen for a snack. Have a pair of scissors handy to cut yourselves loose.

• Find a mentor in someone whose children are grown. Set aside time for a chat with them.

Chapter 2

Assess Our Connectedness

It's hard to be objective when one is caught in a series of family time traps or to be objective when one feels rushed and overwhelmed by daily responsibilities. The following survey and follow-up discussion guide can help you and your family create a realistic picture of what you're doing well as a family, and it suggests areas that could use more attention.

Use the survey that starts on the next page to measure the extent to which your lifestyle choices for good or ill are affecting your family connectedness. For the purposes of this evaluation, "work" refers to all employment, homemaking, and volunteer activities. The survey is intended to be taken by the adults in the family, either individually or together. You may choose to take the survey as an individual and then take it again thinking for the family as a whole. The chapter concludes with a second survey in discussion form, intended for a family conversation.

For each question, enter a number from 0 to 4 in the blank, indicating: (0) Never, (1) Rarely, (2) Sometimes, (3) Regularly, or (4) Frequently. Then add up your total score and read the interpretation of scores following the survey. Be as open and honest as possible; there is great value in naming one's strengths as well as one's growth areas.

The survey may be too weighty for young people. A conversation guided by some excellent questions might work better (see page 22).

Family Time Trap Survey

Time Management

____ Family members spend the right amount of time together and apart.

____ I/We limit the number of activities in which family members participate.

____ I/We use time in a way that makes family a priority.

____ I/We make time for enjoyable activities.

____ My/Our use of time matches my/our personal gifts and talents.

____ I/We can identify where I/we need help managing time.

____ I/We get enough sleep.

____ I/We get enough exercise.

____ I/We make decisions about my/our time for positive reasons rather than to reduce negative influences.

____ I/We have made an accurate assessment of how I/we spend our time.

____ I/We attend to things in a timely way.

"Stuff" (Possessions) Management

____ I am/We are able to delay instant gratification for a long-term goal.

____ I/We do not overspend.

____ I/We reduce the "stuff" I/we collect on a regular basis.

____ I am/We are able to strip away nonessentials as needed.

____ My/Our lifestyle choices enhance my/our marriage and love relationships.

____ I/We demonstrate self-discipline in my/our daily choices.

Work/Daily Chores

____ I/We have an effective method of prioritizing daily activities.

____ I am/we are good at delegating tasks to others.

____ Work has an appropriate place in my/our lives.

____ My/Our work is fulfilling.

____ I/We can leave work behind and focus on my/our family relationships.

____ Household chores are shared equally among members according to age and ability.

____ I/We make lifestyle adjustments as needed.

Spiritual Life

____ I/We take daily time for inner rebuilding through a devotional life.

____ I/We pay attention to my/our longings.

____ I/We worship regularly with other believers.

____ I/We pause to enjoy beautiful things when I/we come upon them.

____ I/We can ask for help when I/we need it.

____ I/We take regular time for confessing sins.

____ My/Our prayers deal with real-life issues.

Attitude

____ I/We compliment others who make family a priority.

____ I /We see myself/ourselves as hopeful.

____ I/We read articles about family issues.

____ I/We believe the best days are yet to come.

_____ I am/We are longing for health and balance.

_____ I am/We are committed to making healthy lifestyle changes.

_____ I am/We are able to share control and decision making with others.

_____ I/We can express my/our feelings easily.

_____ I am/We are quick to smile and laugh.

_____ I am/We are satisfied with most aspects of my/our life/lives.

Free/Recreational Time

_____ Sometimes I/we go on an overnight getaway for fun.

_____ We have at least one activity that everyone likes to do.

_____ I/We celebrate important events.

_____ I/We create events to celebrate.

_____ We have a game closet and use it.

_____ We take regular family vacations.

_____ We entertain on a regular basis.

_____ Our family laughs a lot.

Support

_____ I/We have people outside the family unit that I/we think of as family.

_____ I/We feel well supported by all members of the family.

_____ We attend important events in each other's life.

_____ When one family member has a busy day, others step in to take up the slack.

_____ I/We take personal retreats as needed.

_____ Key people in my/our life/lives support my/our desire for change.

_____ I/We have friends who share similar family values.

____ I/we grew up around people who put a high value on family time.

____ I/we can tell family members when I am/we are feeling overstressed.

Flexibility

____ I am/We are able to admit when I am/we are wrong.

____ I am/We are able to adapt when needed to achieve individual and family goals.

____ I/We have clear goals in life.

____ I/We can persist toward a goal even when difficulties arise.

____ I/We respect family members' need for privacy.

____ I am/We are able to identify and limit unhealthy aspects of my/our life.

____ I/We keep my/our promises.

____ I/We avoid making decisions just to please others.

____ I/We take time to listen to significant issues even when they come at inconvenient times.

____ I/we listen well.

____ I/we strive for a balance of stability and change.

____ Interruptions by a family member don't usually bother me/us.

Daily Life

____ I am/We are organized.

____ I/We have healthy ways of dealing with stress.

____ I/We have healthy ways of dealing with anger.

____ I/We can say no when asked to do things I/we don't want to do at the time.

____ I/We can let the phone ring.

_____ Family members agree on family rules.

_____ There are clear and fair consequences when family rules aren't followed.

_____ Our family limits the amount of time spent watching television, working or playing on the computer, etc.

_____ I am/We are comfortable with the amount of meals the family shares together.

_____ We have written a family covenant.

_____ **TOTAL SCORE**

Interpretation of Your Total Score

240–320 points: You typically do a fine job avoiding family time traps. Well done! Spend some time affirming those around you. You might be able to improve things a bit here and a bit there, but overall you're an inspiration to those who know you well. (You're probably reading this book to reaffirm many things you've already learned, or because you're concerned about others.) Share your accumulated wisdom with others as necessary. We have found that people who enjoy talking about the issues in this book seek us out and initiate conversations with us. When you choose to share your personal story and insights about your lifestyle with others, focus on the grace and freedom that come from growing in good choices rather than using dialogue-terminating phrases such as "You really ought to. . . ." Your story will stand on its own; let your friends draw their own conclusions from it for their own lives.

190–239 points: Many aspects of your family life are on track. Take time to name and celebrate the positive aspects of your family life with your loved ones. Then consider setting a few new goals to address the growth areas. Pay special attention to the kinds of questions that you answered with a 1 or a 4.

Do you see a common theme among these questions? We're always moving toward healthier living or away from it. You have a good process going. Keep it up, and share your journey with others as they express an interest.

140–189 points: You are probably longing for some significant changes in how your family lives, though there are reasons here and there to be content. Rejoice where things are going well. But remember that longing for things to change is the first step in making healthier choices. Check with your family members and interested friends to see if your assessments are accurate. Some people have a tendency to make things seem better than they really are, some worse. Don't be afraid to ask family members and friends for help in moving things in a better direction. If they join you in your journey, you're likely to join them in theirs!

50–139 points: Your score indicates a strong need to make lasting changes for your personal life and the good of your family. Today could be a turning point for you. As you go over your answers, you might be tempted to feel discouraged. But know this: facing your needs honestly is the beginning of making the changes that you've been longing for. There is no shortcut for this process. It often takes inner pain to bring about outer change. The support of a group of like-minded people would be a tremendous asset to you right now. Could you take up this book for discussion and support with a small group of friends? Is there an appropriate forum for study and discussion at your church?

0–49 points: This survey is a sketchy reflection of what is going on in your heart and mind. It is possible that you are hurting quite badly right now. You may need more than a discussion or support group can offer. Consider calling your pastor or a counselor to begin a process that can get you back on track. God bless you on your journey.

The questions below are based on Dolores Curran's book *Traits of a Healthy Family*.[1] She has identified fifteen traits that healthy families share, though it is not likely that any family enjoys all fifteen. Let the questions guide your family in organizing discussion and making gentle changes where necessary.

1. When do we communicate and listen to each other best?

2. When have you felt affirmed and supported by other family members?

3. What are some ways we can show even greater respect for each other?

4. What experiences have taught us to trust each other?

5. Can you share a memory of a funny family time?

6. How does a family share responsibilities?

7. How do we know what's right and what's wrong?

8. Which of our family traditions are worth passing on to others?

9. Why is each person's input important to our family?

10. Why is faith in God important to our family?

11. How do we respect each other's privacy?

12. What can we do as a family to help others?

13. What can we do to share more meals together and talk more with each other?

14. What plans do we have to spend our time off together?

15. When we have problems as a family, whom might we call for some help?

The surveys in this chapter provide a snapshot of how your family is living today. If they have caused you to long for something new in your family, perhaps you're ready to "come clean." If so, the next chapter was written especially for you.

Part II

What Is Stopping Us from Connecting?

Chapter 3

Time Burglars

Over and over again we have heard it: "If we just had more time . . ."; "There isn't enough time . . ."; "I only have so much time. . . ." Something is stealing our time, and we all are getting a little tired of playing the victim. We need to identify the time burglars in our lives and put them out of business. Let's take a look at some realistic ways to conquer those time criminals and reclaim some of that stolen time for family.

One can draw an analogy between overspending finances and overspending time. Both money and time have one thing in common: limits. In the case of time, there are limits to how much can be squeezed into a twenty-four-hour period. It doesn't matter what you call it—quality time, free time, down time, peak hours—time still has to fit within a budget: an unmovable twenty-four-hour budget that won't budge unless you want to shortchange yourself on sleep. Sooner or later, you have to pay up.

When we stop to analyze our time dilemma, we might be surprised to find that we do not have enough family time because we've already spent it. We've overcommitted ourselves to other well-deserving projects or activities. We've overburdened ourselves with too many responsibilities. We spend our remaining family time trying to recoup lost sleep or unwind by zoning out in front of the TV or the computer.

A lot of the time being stolen isn't someone else's fault. The hole is in our own pocket.

But where to start? It helps to get a handle on just where time is being spent. For a week or two, keep a time journal of how your day breaks down. Write down your activities for each hour of the day. Have your spouse do the same. Encourage your children, if they are old enough, to carry their own time diary, or keep track of their after-school hours for them. At the end of a week or two, compare notes.

What do you notice? How much of your time has already been spent before you even get up? How much free time do you actually have? What decisions could you make to regain some control over those parts of your day? Share with your family your concerns over how you each spend your time.

When we asked families to identify specific areas that they felt robbed them of family time, many gave the same answers:

1. household chores
2. habitual TV watching
3. overscheduling

Perhaps your family can identify with these answers. Doing something about each of them is not insurmountable. We can take back the time that is rightfully ours. We can start the day with time to spare and have enough left over at the end to hear our child's prayers without falling asleep on their pillow. In the end, it really doesn't matter how much time we've spent but with whom we've spent it. It's the old connecting thing. Now, let's get busy. We've got burglars to catch.

Household Chores

If you have two cars, you have two cars that need washing, gas, oil, tires, and insurance. If you've got a living room and a family room, that's double the vacuuming and twice the space for other stuff to start piling up. If you've got forty pairs of socks in your laundry basket and none in your drawers, it's probably because it takes a lot longer to match forty pairs than it does to match ten. It's elementary: the more you have, the more you have to take care of.

Do a simple experiment. Gather the troops and a couple of laundry baskets. Point them to their rooms and tell them to come back with stuff they really don't need. You know the rules: If it hasn't been worn in a year—into the basket. If you can't remember the last time you played, watched, or listened to it—into the basket. If it doesn't have sentimental value and you really can't remember who gave it to you anyway—into the basket. Set a time limit and send each person off to collect. When the timer goes off, hop in the car and deliver the goods to your local thrift store. No reneging. Go home and appreciate all that you still have. That's good family time.

Kids with less stuff have cleaner rooms. Three pairs of jeans means that only two can be on the floor at one time—they have to wear one, right? The same goes for sweatshirts, jackets, mittens. We appreciate one when it's the only one we have, and things tend to receive better care when there's not another one to back it up.

Think about the "time tax" next time you purchase an item. How much time will it cost to maintain this item? Does this item really save time or just complicate an already cluttered cleaning supply closet? Is there a place for this item or will it squeeze in next to three others just like it. A friend once told us she had seven sets of measuring spoons!

Once in a while, we spend time at a monastery. We're always given a clean room with a desk, bed, chair, and reading lamp. And we're always amazed at how free we feel surrounded by fewer possessions. In the morning, it takes just minutes to straighten the room and make the bed, and we're off with time to spare.

Everybody has weak points. Kate's CD collection has taken over her bedroom. David is addicted to thriller novels, books on backgammon, and Macintosh computers. Reed has more than his share of chess books, boards, and trophies. Jill likes art supplies and has filled up several storage boxes with paper and interesting stuff. I (Barbara) have several tubes of lipstick scattered around the house and in purses—but I can never find one in a hurry. It's not just a matter of getting rid of stuff. These things aren't inherently evil. Catching this time burglar is about getting rid of unnecessary stuff, the items that get in the way of enjoying our real possessions.

What's your weak point? How many multiples do you have in your closet, on your shelves, or piled up in a corner somewhere? Stuff takes time—time to maintain, time to pick up, time to store and retrieve. If you have seven sets of measuring spoons, can you find anything else in that drawer? It's your call. You decide when enough is enough.

Even when we've pared down and simplified, there's still the matter of chores, things that just have to be done, such as washing clothes, preparing meals, taking out the garbage. This may be a hard sell, but chores, especially shared chores, can be great family time. Find some lively music, set the timer for twenty minutes, establish the goal, and move, move, move! Reward yourself when you've finished the unpleasant task. Shared work turns an isolated job into a celebration. Smaller children especially love to feel the sense of belonging that comes with working together.

Look back at your time journals and count up the minutes each family member spends taking care of the day-to-day stuff that keeps a family running smoothly. Sit down as a family and ask each other if the housework is shared fairly. How could you reorganize the workload so that some chores become shared family time? What chores are you doing that really belong to someone else? Resolve to make a change where needed. Set a time to meet again and check on your progress. Keep one another accountable.

This time burglar is a "no-brainer." Keep things simple. If the cupboards are full, get rid of things until you have more space than you need. If you bring home something new, share something old with someone else. You'll be amazed how liberating it is to open a drawer and see what you're looking for without having to hunt for it.

Putting simple limits on things and sharing the workload create extra moments that add up into hours spent with those we love instead of looking for the hammer or scissors or glue or tape. Reclaim lost time by living with less. Share the work. Reap the benefits. Think about it.

Connecting Points

• Read back over the suggested activities in this section. Pull out one or two ideas and see what progress you can make in a week. Enlist the help of all family members. Set a family goal to eliminate "stuff" in one area of your home by a certain time. When your goal is reached, celebrate with a movie or other special activity. Enjoy the time you recovered by living with less.

• Encourage other families in your church or neighborhood to clean out a closet or two on the same day. At the church or agreed-upon home, put kids to work boxing and bagging what you've managed to discard. You may find that someone else's hand-me-down meets a need at your home or vice versa. Together, bring the clothing and other items to a Salvation Army or thrift store. Meet together for potluck or a simple meal and give thanks for work shared.

Habitual TV Watching

According to the National Institute on Media and the Family, TV takes up the biggest amount of awake time of the average American child. The average child spends half an hour alone with father, two and one-half hours alone with mother, five hours on homework, two hours reading, and twenty-four hours watching television per week.[1] That's more than a half-time job.

Take a TV inventory at your home. Are your kids among the 56 percent of American school-age children with TV sets in their bedrooms? If so, do you think that could interfere with family time? Do we hear the sound of parental feet marching toward a child's room to remove the number one obstacle in the quest for more family time? Children may whine at first. Remain unyielding. Practice saying, "If we're going to watch TV, we're going to watch it together or at least be in the same room!"

The family is bombarded by TV and other media. A workshop we attended asked participants to list ten to fifteen things they did in a week that didn't involve media or some kind of computer screen. When we're looking at a screen, be it TV, computer, or a big movie screen, it's hard to look at anyone else. How many of us have experienced interrupting someone's game or program with some really great news only to be met with "Shhhh!" If we're looking to connect, maybe we need to think about disconnecting from some of the devices technology has brought us. What else might you be doing with that time?

If you're not convinced that showing restraint in TV viewing or computer habits could gain back hours of family time during the course of a week, consider what really runs the big network programming as well as all those Web sites: advertising. It's one big sell job. More than soda, toothpaste, and breakfast cereal is being sold. It has been said that the people who tell the stories create the culture. Who is telling our stories, creating our culture, setting our values? Who are the people—nameless authors, except at TV award times— who mentor our children with their sitcoms and cop shows? Who are the faces behind the Saturday morning commercials who knock on our TV screens and ask for a private showing with our children? We're not used to letting strangers into our home to talk with our kids even when we are at home.

In the book *TV, Becoming Unglued: A Guide to Help Children Develop Positive TV Habits,* a sixth-grader admits, "The week I turned off my television, I read more books, my school grades got a little better, I practiced piano more, I also learned to knit. I played a lot of indoor games with my sister and brothers, I got to know my family and myself better."[2] Amen, little honey! Amen!

In reality, TV is not going away, so best to take time to model some "media smarts" for the kids. TV programs, when viewed together with children, give parents a chance to share some of their own values and reactions to what's on the screen. Developing critical-thinking skills means questioning the actions or choices of a character, presenting alternatives to the story line, pointing out the effect of music and special effects—the list goes on and on.

A lot of value clarification can be done just by responding to what the TV dishes out. A well-timed "I don't buy that!" in response to a commercial or a sarcastic "Now that's realistic!" to a character's actions reaches kids as well as—or better than—a lecture on values. When we watch TV with our kids, we have a chance to dialogue about what we see. We can model the art of flipping channels when a program crosses boundaries the family has set. We can show our kids the "off" button that frees them to do other activities. When it comes to TV, it's good to remember who's in charge of what we watch, when we watch, and how we watch.

Addie Jurs, author of *TV, Becoming Unglued,* provides excellent ideas for parents who want to use TV viewing time to promote family values and help train children to be critical thinkers. Think about ways your family can prevent losing so many hours to unmonitored TV shows. Tape selected shows so that a pause button can be used if you want to stop and talk about something. Don't forget to talk about some of the methods used to sell products during commercial time, too.

Addie Jurs states: "When parents guide their children through the decision-making process and encourage them to be selective TV viewers, they prepare their children to make decisions in the future. Teaching children to question what they see and hear on TV helps young people to become thinking adults. By limiting children to what families decide is the best of TV, parents enrich their children's lives."[3]

So we want more time to connect with our family. Here's the remote. Here's the "off" button. Press it and see what happens!

Connecting Points

• Take a time survey on the amount of TV viewed by each family member. How do your children fare against the national average? Meet as a family and discuss your results. Come up with a plan for TV viewing that everyone can live with. Try out your plan for a week and then meet again to discuss the effects. Make adjustments to the plan, if needed. Keep refining it until you have TV viewing under control.

• Try going for an agreed-upon amount of time without watching any TV. Be prepared for kids to complain that they don't have anything to do. Don't be quick to help them come up with activities. Part of the process of unplugging is dealing with boredom. In time, they will find other activities. At the end of your agreed-upon time, discuss what activities your family or individual family members substituted in place of watching TV. What did you learn from this experiment?

• Check the weekly TV schedule. As a family, decide which programs you will watch together that week. Make it special by preparing a favorite snack. We have fond memories of watching *The Wonderful World of Disney* and sharing a bowl of popcorn every Sunday night with the rest of our family. Create a memory of your own.

Overscheduling

You already know a lot about the overscheduling time burglar. He's familiar, wears a well-intentioned face, tends to sprint between activities, and falls into bed exhausted at the end of the day. This burglar gets impatient when people take too long to tell him something and has trouble putting people before the task at hand. This time burglar never feels quite appreciated for all his efforts, yet he never has time to do a really good job at one thing because so many things have his attention. And as hard as he tries, his efforts never seem quite enough. Yes, the drive to overschedule is sneaky: "But it's all so important"; "Who will do this if I don't?"; "But they really need me!" Like wolves in sheep's clothing, our own good intentions can gobble us up if we aren't careful!

Two women have taught us a lot about scheduling time. One, Janet, is a well-trusted counselor in a small Midwestern town. It seems that everyone, at one time or another, has had a good talk with Janet. She's that kind of person. Whether she's "working" or not, Janet knows how to listen and people respond. But Janet also knows her limitations. Janet's not on a lot of committees. She doesn't do a lot of volunteer work. She once said, "I do my job and I do my home, and that's all I can handle for now."

We met Sonia when we lived in Eau Claire, Wisconsin. Sonia was a Montessori school advocate and literally took us by the hand and dragged us into a classroom so we could see for ourselves. All three of our kids attended a Montessori preschool because of that visit.

Advocacy was just one of Sonia's gifts. Upon meeting us for the first time, she asked if we were "arty." She wasn't trying to be pretentious. She loved the arts, any kind, and was always looking for a comrade who shared her passion. But, with all her gifts, Sonia was very selective in sharing them. She was not one to say yes very often. We were both working in the church at the time and always looking for volunteers.

Sonia said no more than we wanted to hear. We didn't understand that until we went to one of Sonia's "yes events."

It was the kind of event that one goes to and afterward says, "That was wonderful." Years later, we still remember Sonia's efforts on that special program and remain awed. Maybe it was her Montessori experience, but she just didn't create a program that evening, she created an environment. Backdrops, lighting, sound, well-chosen readings, poetry, music. We all left inspired. When Sonia said yes, she meant it.

Too often we find our own efforts lacking, ending up with a mediocre product that does the job but doesn't reflect our best work. We settle because it's the best we can do, considering our other commitments. Sometimes it's a hurried supper with little time to touch base during the day. Other times it's an important conversation cut short because we "had to go." At those times, we think of Janet and Sonia. Learning to say no to outside commitments means that when we say yes, we give it our best shot. Learning to say no doesn't mean we're saying "No, never," just "No, not now." Learning to say no means that we understand that we are not perfect and have limits to our time and energy.

Think about your commitments. Think about the commitments your children and spouse have made. Sometimes we model family life after the airlines, overbooking our days and hoping for "no-shows" so we can fit everything in. That is not a good model. Sooner or later, somebody gets bumped. Usually, it is those who love us the most and we know will understand. We never like that when it happens.

If you had to cut your present commitments down to two, what would they be? What activities would your children choose? Think about scaling back your commitments to give more time to your top two choices. There might be some grieving in the process, some ego reduction, but it will be temporary.

It's good to know what one can handle. It's also good to remember that there is a "time for every purpose under heaven" (Ecclesiastes 3:1). If we want more family time, some choices need to be made; some of us need to make radical readjustments in our thinking. Overscheduling gives a lot of us the illusion of self-worth. It can keep us too busy to ask the important questions. Overscheduling stops us from really getting involved in our primary commitments and relationships. We need to ask ourselves why, but reflection—well, reflection takes time, and that's a problem. It's time to take the time. Ask the hard questions and be gentle on yourself when the answers come. A family's lifestyle is not a matter of stringing a bunch of shoulds together and feeling guilty when you fall short. There is a God in the midst of your family whose gift to you is grace, unconditional love, and real self-worth.

The next time you are asked to make a commitment, ask yourself these questions before you respond:

1. Is this the right activity for this time in my life?

2. How will this commitment affect the other commitments I have already made to job and family?

3. Am I able to give this commitment a full yes?

4. Am I saying yes for the right reasons?

If you find your responses coming up short, practice saying what a newfound friend taught us: "I'm sorry. This just does not work for me right now." It's a gentle response that requires no further explanation and leaves you with a manageable schedule with time for all that's important to you.

Connecting Points

• What time mentors do you have in your life right now? What are they doing right? What do you admire about them?

• On a scale of 1 to 10, how hurried is your family? Who or what sets the pace for how fast your family runs?

• Plan a long car ride with your family and ban all portable CD players and earphones. This is time to talk. Discuss your family's schedule. Listen to what people are saying. Make adjustments where needed.

• Think about limiting family members' activities. We have a loose rule allowing family members two evenings out each week and another that all members will be present for supper or have an acceptable reason for not to attending. Like all limits, there are weeks where the rules get stretched, but now, instead of running faster, we stop and try to recoup that time later. Everyone knows the expectation and works toward the common goal. Setting limits can be liberating and gives family members permission to say no to outside commitments when necessary.

Chapter 4

Work

Ever since World War II, when women left the home front and marched into the magical world of work outside the home, they have been trying to redefine the boundaries between work and home. Long hours at work mean fewer hours at home. The remaining time at home must accommodate all housework, shopping, and home repairs yet still leave room to be patient with children and meet their needs. In more than one household, when we try to make a connection, we're likely to get a busy signal.

As people have realized that the notion of a "supermom" is a myth, a growing number of husbands have braved the gender lines and learned to do what used to be called "women's work." But even in our present, more enlightened state, we still hear a lot of confusion on the topic of work, especially from women.

A common response to the work/home dilemma goes something like this: "I'd like to stay home, but I don't know how we would manage it financially." Or, "I'd like to stay home, but I think it would drive me crazy. I need more stimulation than my two-year-old can offer."

Family connectedness is created by frequent, meaningful contact. This is difficult when both parents are working long hours. This chapter should help you clarify the reasons people choose to work and offer a process for finding a good balance between the need or desire to work and the desire to connect with family.

Even though we try to be integrated about our priorities and values, we all do a certain amount of bluffing. This was eloquently addressed in an article in *U.S. News and World Report*, "Lies Parents Tell Themselves about Why They Work."[1] The article looks at the reasons people give for shortchanging family with work. You would probably recognize many of the comments reported, having heard them from your own mouth as well as from others who work to balance family and career. The writers identify three core myths many of us share:

> *Myth 1:* "We both work because we need the money."
>
> *Myth 2:* "It's OK for both of us to work because our child is in good day care."
>
> *Myth 3:* "If only companies were more flexible, I'd spend more time with my kids."

It's easy to get defensive about this, starting with the rationale about having no choice in the matter. But that's just another bluff. We always have choices when it comes to managing our time. We need to look at how our own past lifestyle choices may have denied us the ability to make more flexible decisions now. We may need to ask ourselves if there are ways to undo some of the decisions that keep us locked into a regimented workweek with little room for improvement.

So let's try to untangle fact from assumption, truth from wishful thinking, myth from reality. "Coming clean" is a good first step toward dismantling the family time trap.

Myth 1: "We both work because we need the money."

What do we really need? Needs and wants can be very slippery things. In our early thirties,we wrestled with the want versus need question as a couple both of us then sharing the responsibilities of a demanding job at a large church in Eau Claire,

Wisconsin. But anyone who has ever worked part-time, especially for the church, knows the job doesn't stay part-time very long. The more hours we put in, the higher the bills seemed to go. When time got tight, we used some of the extra money to buy convenience. And that's where the rub came. What felt like a necessity often was just a consequence of our own choice to put in those extra hours. A common theme.

According to "Lies Parents Tell Themselves about Why They Work," the rub comes no matter what one's income bracket is. The article quotes a 1996 survey in which "people with high incomes were just as likely to say they worked for 'basic necessities' as were those at the economic margins."[2] But necessities have become upwardly mobile, like everything else in the past few decades.

> When asked in a 1975 survey to define "the good life," a majority listed only a handful of things: a car, a lawn, and home they owned; a happy marriage; an interesting job; and being able to afford college for their kids. Twenty years later, the Roper Starch Worldwide survey found that most respondents defined "the good life" to mean far more in material terms: a job that pays "much more than average," "a lot of money," a color TV. Four in ten [respondents] added "really nice clothes," a second car, a vacation home, travel abroad. Thirty-seven percent even mentioned a swimming pool.[3]

Add to this the fact that Americans are twice as productive now as they were in the 1940s. The thirty-hour workweek, once touted as the cure-all for stressed-out workers, could be a reality if we're willing to live at the same standard of living as people in the 1940s. Back then, the norm was one car and one garage, and you did your dishes by hand.

Wants versus needs. Necessity versus those little extras. What price are we willing to pay in order to have the basics? How big does a house really have to be? How much stuff is enough? When is a car too old? Slippery questions, but who has the time to think about them? It's much easier to lament our lack of choice in the matter and go on our way as usual.

On the other hand, a growing number of couples have stopped and thought about it. A recent headline on the front page of a Minnesota newspaper read, "Paring Parents' Work-week Helps Kids."[4] Called the "Four-Thirds Solution," an idea laid out by Stanley Greenspan, psychologist and professor at George Washington University in Washington, D.C., parents would each cut their working hours to two-thirds. This "family-friendly approach to careers" gives the family more than one income and allows parents more time to be home with their children. The plan's willingness to treat both careers equally has been applauded, but others argue that four-thirds of an income still isn't enough to meet needs. Still, it adds another choice to recent efforts to rearrange the traditional workweek.

Part of a decision to cut back on work, or not, is just basic economics. It's the extras that take a bite out of that paycheck. Working can be expensive. Child care, a work wardrobe, eating out, taxes, and household help are necessities if both parents choose to work. We all need to stop and figure out how much we're really taking home for the family to cover the basic necessities and how much goes out as a consequence of the job. Then we need to ask ourselves if it is worth it.

Connecting Points

• If there is a stay-at-home parent in your family, pick a whole week or month in which to honor that person. Challenge yourself to find creative (rather than costly) ways to honor that person and say thank you on a daily basis for all she or he does.

• Set aside an evening to get a figure on just what it's costing your family to have two careers. Do you carry double insurance from both jobs? Are there union dues for full-time employers that would be cut if you worked part-time? Draw a line down the middle of a paper and list the pros and the cons of your job in the appropriate column. If you are feeling uneasy about making a change, try to name the feeling. Once it is named, you'll know where to go from there.

Myth 2: "It's OK for both of us to work because our child is in good day care."

If you have or have had a child in day care, it might be tempting to put the book down at this point. We know; we've been there. We never found any easy answers either.

I (Barbara) had been home for two years with our oldest and daughters Kate and Jill when we were asked to consider working as a husband-and-wife team at a large Lutheran church in Eau Claire, Wisconsin. With David's clergy background and my teaching experience, this education position seemed perfect. We would share the child care, and share household responsibilities.

It didn't take long before we both felt the need to be at the same meetings and our hours began to overlap. We decided to look for some occasional day care and were delighted to find that the church had rented space to a licensed business. Our kids could go with us to work. I'm sure they were thrilled.

We were rushing a lot back then. We were rushing one day to get both girls ready and to the church in time for a staff meeting. I hurriedly told the supervisors the girls' names, gave the kids a quick kiss, pointed at all the toys, and said, "Have fun!" Actually, it was I who was going to "have fun"! Kate and Jill, at ages three and one, were having their lives altered. I'm not proud of my insensitivity.

Later, as I was going out to the car for some forgotten papers, I heard loud wailing from the upstairs windows. I recognized the sound of our "big girl," Kate, in distress. Her face was red and puffy. She had been crying for a while. She did not want to lie down for "nap time" on strange plastic mats with twenty other kids she didn't know. I wouldn't have wanted to either. I stayed with her until she was calm and then went back to that all-important meeting. I don't remember what we discussed that day, but I still remember Kate's face.

I share this story not to fan the flames of guilt that working mothers and a growing number of working fathers often carry but because it shows how easy it is to say "family first" and then fall back into old patterns. Family first requires a reordering of priorities, a reminder that someone else besides our kids might have to wait. Not all bosses will understand. When a teacher friend of ours went to her principal for part-time hours because her workload cut too deeply into her weekend and time with family, his response came just short of calling her unprofessional.

The Old Testament version of this work/home dilemma is referred to as "serving two gods." Difficult though it is, sometimes we just have to choose.

Dale Williams, a school social worker and a parent who has bought into Greenspan's Four-Thirds Solution, said the following: "My philosophy is, to be happy you have to define your own dream. The career ladder is someone else's dream. So if it is hurting my career, so be it."[5]

We all want to be good parents and do what's right for our kids. But parenting is confusing. There are a lot of mixed messages out there, and self-actualization doesn't always mix well with family responsibilities. Add to that a raging debate over the pros and cons of day care and the answer to the home/work quandary gets even more unclear. Although some studies show that attentive parents who send their two- or three-year-olds to high-quality day care could be boosting their children's cognitive and language skills, those kids still need someone to talk to when they get home.

Always well prepared, my parents have made arrangements for their funerals and gravestone. In spite of many the personal accomplishments they made during their working years, they have decided to write the following on their gravestone (note: David is also Barbara's brother's name):

> William and Joyce DeGrote
> Parents of David and Barbara

Harvey F. Egan, pastor emeritus of Saint Joan of Arc Church in Minneapolis, reached a similar conclusion about his priorities. On reaching his eightieth year, he quoted a friend who was the same age: "In the evening, we see that what we are is more important than what we do—and *whose* we are is most important."[6]

Take a walk through a cemetery. What you will see are the relationships: "Wife of . . . husband of . . . daughter, son." In the end, it's the connections we value most. Everything else is just a golden calf.

Connecting Points

• Challenge your family's assumptions about the need for day care. Look for ways to be more flexible with your work/home hours. Consider some of the many choices we now have for dealing with our work hours. If you need to use full-time day care, be honest about your reasons.

• You might brainstorm some ideas with your church family. Could a few well-placed rides by church volunteer drivers or a "latch key" program to care for children offer needed flexibility to working parents?

Myth 3: "If only companies were more flexible, I'd spend more time with my kids."

The words are all there: *flex time, part-time, job share, tele-commuting, work at home.* If flexibility is what we want, polit-ically correct companies have responded; even the most hard-nosed company doesn't want to be seen putting busi-ness before family. Yes, the programs are sometimes there. But are we using them when we find them?

In "Confessions of an Advertising Man," David Ogilvy observes, "If you stay home and tend your gardens and chil-dren, I will love you more as a human being, but don't expect to be the first person promoted in your group."[7] Opting for more creative arrangements for balancing home and family that put family first can, in Ogilvy's words, be "lousy for your career." *U.S. News and World Report* cited several stories of people using more creative job choices who were "typically more efficient and productive" than their nine-to-five col-leagues, and yet they were often "downgraded for showing less than 100 percent commitment to [the] job."[8] It appears that when management doesn't see your face, it seems to think that you don't care.

But lack of support from management may not be what's really going on here. Sociologist Arlie Hoshschild concluded that for some, being at work is easier than being at home:

> Home life has become more like an efficiently run but joyless workplace, while the actual workplace with its new emphasis on empowerment and teamwork is more like a family. Among employees she [Hoshschild] observed home had become a place filled with incessant demands from noisy children, endless piles of laundry, few tangible rewards and little time to relax. At work, by contrast, people felt in control. They knew what was expected of them, and their hard work was appreciated by colleagues and supervisors.[9]

Family responsibilities aren't always fun, and it's easy to see how work can become a "haven" from some of the daily, unrelenting responsibilities that make up a large part of our at-home life.

What has taken the joy out of family life so that we would prefer the company of colleagues to the company of each other? Where is the appreciation for the little things? Why aren't we laughing? Is it possible that we have learned to define ourselves more by what we do than by whom we love? Have we become human doings instead of human beings?

In some ways it's easier to get up, put on the work clothes, shut the door, and head off to work. Going and doing have become the mantra for success. But people are learning that there's a cost: disconnectedness, depression, separation from those who have been placed in our lives to care for us and give us joy as we care for them and try to do right by them. We end up tired, stressed, and often alone. Is putting in those extra couple of hours at the desk really worth it?

Building a strong family takes time. You can't buy it—it's time you spend, not money. More and more of us are realizing that even though we may want both time and money, we can't easily have both. And so the choice becomes: Which do we want more—time or money?

Connecting Points

• In what ways could your money buy time? Could you hire someone to do your yard work, clean your house, tackle the garage, or deliver your groceries? If you choose to keep some of your work hours, how can you use the extra income to buy back family time?

• If you could create your family lifestyle with fewer restrictions on your choices, how would you choose to live? Although you might not be able to snap your fingers and make it all happen, you do have some choices—probably more than you have considered. Without building false hopes, try to amend your present situation in the direction of your longings. (A church youth group used this planning process to decide on where to spend Christmas vacation. Although they longed to take a Boeing 747 to the Bahamas, they settled for taking a bus to a large metro area to hang out at a spa and sports facility. It wasn't everything they wanted, but it got them planning in the right direction.)

* * * * *

Let's look at some numbers. According to *Focus on the Family,* in the early 1990s, parents spent 40 percent less time with their children than they did twenty-five years earlier. In 1965, average parents spent about thirty hours a week with their children. By 1991, the average parent spent seventeen hours. What has been cut from our lives with that 40-percent reduction of family time? "Little League games, birthday parties, evenings, weekends, shared lunch hours, gardening, reading, movies and most other pastimes."[10] These are the things of which families are made, things that keep us feeling valued, loved, and connected.

We've found that working keeps us independent, confident, and able to survive just fine, thank you. It improves our lifestyles and buys us lots of stuff. It allows us to give things to our loved ones whether they want them or not. "I work for life's necessities," we say. But maybe it is closer to the truth that we work to have the excesses of life and thereby fall headlong into the family time trap. Sometimes we just have to go back and undo what we've done, take a really close look at our needs and wants, and, when necessary, ask forgiveness and start again.

If you need to do so, repent, which means literally to turn around and go the other way. It's often the point at which God begins the best work in our lives.

Part III

How Can We Create Connectedness?

Chapter 5

Create a Family Covenant

Scan a bookshelf on family issues at a favorite bookstore or library and it won't take long to find the word *strong*. Maybe *strong* is such a popular word because so many of us are feeling rather weak in view of the family bonds broken by unshared activity, rushed meals, and interrupted conversation. It's a familiar story.

What makes a family strong? Popular authors on family-related topics, such as Dolores Curran or Steven Covey, often list strengths, habits, or traits found in families that seem to be in the groove. If we were to take all the lists drawn up by the wisest writers on this topic and boil them down into one sentence, it might look something like this: Strong families are families who have a clear image of who they are.

This image develops slowly as events and attitudes are repeated over and over, making their way into the infrastructure of the family so quietly that, without reflection, we might not even recognize it. Such family rituals keep us connected and help define what it means to be who we are as a family.

We propose a family covenant, as this is more than just an agreement between members of the family, more than just a New Year's resolution, easily conceived, easily broken. *The Interpreter's Dictionary of the Bible* says that a *covenant* is "a solemn promise . . . recognized by [all] parties as the formal act which binds the actor[s] to fulfill [their] promise."

If the members of the covenant family are wrung out by unhealthy habits and attitudes, however, especially regarding the use of their time, they are likely, without direction, to create a covenant process something like this: "I need you to be more respectful to me"; "Oh, yeah? I need you to stay away from my stuff"; "I need time away from you all"; "Maybe we all need a vacation"; "Yeah, right, who has the time?"

Allow us to offer some guidelines in creating a family covenant. It won't do for a parent to throw together a few quick sentences in ten minutes and then spoon-feed them to the others. The process described in this chapter is more like a journey down memory lane, filled with excursions into remembrances past, the sharing of personal treasures, talking about things that matter, and planning for a more hopeful future together while sharing mutual affirmation and love. The destination—a covenant between the members of your family—is only part of the payoff. The process itself is an irreplaceable facet of the promises you make to each other. This will be major connecting time. The time you spend with each other creating this covenant is part of what heals your family's hurry sickness. You've heard it said, "Time heals all wounds." Don't believe it for a minute. But time well spent can head you in the right direction.

We're assuming that someone who has read this book is facilitating the covenant process. That doesn't mean that you have all the answers; it means that you are willing to keep things moving in a good direction.

Guidelines

When the family is together, invite everyone to pull out their calendars and—this might be the hardest part of all—find three hours in which you can meet to create your family covenant. Set three separate one-hour "dates"; if anyone from outside the family tries to take away any of those hours, you can explain, "Sorry, can't do that with you then, I have a date." Each of the three dates will deal with a special topic: (1) we are; (2) we believe; and (3) we covenant. The best alternative would be to meet on three different days for one hour each time (larger families may need more time), with several days between each date. Three Sunday early evenings in a row might work well. In a pinch, you could do it all in one afternoon, but the results will be better if, like a fine cup of tea, you allow things to steep between family meetings. That will allow minds to grasp what is experienced and come better prepared for the next date. Keep in mind the needs of family members who have trouble focusing for longer periods of time. Avoid late evenings, if possible; break the process into six half-hour segments, if necessary.

When you meet to set dates, be sure to ask each family member to prepare for the first date by collecting a handful of personal items and photographs that say something about who your family is. Explain that the family is going to put the items together in such a way that even a stranger could learn a lot about who the family is. Items might include something out of a bedroom or closet, sports and hobby equipment, books, pictures from a favorite vacation or family time, something precious, something funny, and a wall hanging or a special item from a shelf. Choose items that reflect the family's group identity, but items that describe each individual are fine, too. Remember, a family is made up of individuals who are each unique.

In advance, get a large candle (perhaps four inches in diameter and a foot high). This will be lit during the three dates, and then during a meal each day thereafter, until the candle is used up. This could take weeks or months. Retiring the covenant candle will signal that it's time to review the family covenant, to celebrate the positive outcomes of the covenant, and make any necessary adjustments to the family promises.

Also, have at least six large sheets of tagboard (two each of three different light colors would work best, as will be explained), a Bible (a version that's relatively easy for everyone to understand), one or two markers, scissors for everyone, glue or Scotch tape, and enough old magazines for each person to have a few (remember to share the work gathering these items). You will be cutting pictures and words out of the magazines and securing them to the tagboard.

This process is intended to be a positive experience, but don't get discouraged if it takes younger family members some time before settling into it. Keep a positive, grace-filled attitude. Try not to let one or two people dominate or control too much of the process. Find a way to include everyone. They will have a sense of their thoughts and feelings being valued, and they will have a stake in the outcome, a heightened sense of co-ownership of the end result: your family covenant.

Note: If your family is so stressed or unhappy that you can't easily move in the same direction for three hours, consider leaving your family covenant for another time. Leaders of Marriage Encounter say their program is geared not to providing therapy to a hurting marriage but "to make a good marriage better." Similarly, building a family covenant is too difficult if members are not at least heading in roughly the same direction. Calling a truce if some family members seem modestly out of sorts with each other might work. But if you must bail out during the process, set a future date to get back to it, and take time to mend relationships sufficiently to try it again. Don't hesitate to seek out family counseling as a preliminary step in this process. Most people go through times when they need professional counseling; the winners are not those who hide their hurts for appearance sake, but those who deal honestly with their needs.

The First Date: We Are . . .

Meet comfortably in a circle so that everyone can easily see everyone else. Sitting at a kitchen table or dining room table will do nicely, because the first two dates will include cutting and gluing.

Light the covenant candle and take time to acclimatize to your together time by sharing. Our family frequently does this at suppertime in a session we call Good Thing/Bad Thing: each person relates briefly a "good" thing that has happened recently, or a "bad" thing, or both. It is surprising how often "good" things have negative elements and "bad" things have some redeeming value. Consider holding a Good Thing/Bad Thing session daily at a family meal. Take time to celebrate or commiserate a bit with each person's sharing. This practice has been a great blessing for our family.

Move now to sharing the personal items that family members have chosen to help characterize your family. On the top of one of the sheets of tagboard, write, "We Are. . . ." As the items are introduced, have one person be the "scribe," jotting down on the tagboard what is shared; these thoughts are not likely to be in one place ever again!

Next, hand out magazines and scissors, asking each family member to cut out pictures, words, and phrases from the magazines that remind them of your family. After each person has cut out a handful of items, have each one share what the pictures and words mean to them as they are glued or taped to another sheet of the same-colored tagboard that also has "We Are . . ." written at the top.

Now that your family has started with some good, hands-on activities, take time to discuss the following questions (the scribe should take notes on the back of the tagboard sheets):

• What item do you wish you could have shared but didn't (e.g., "I wish we had a photo of . . ."; "I didn't find a picture of this in a magazine, but we could add . . .")?

- If a stranger were to look at the items we shared today, what would they tell him or her about our family?

- What do the items and clippings say about how our family uses time? (Include both the positive and the negative.)

- What might we consider doing differently that would help our family when we are bitten by the hurry-up bug?

- What one thing can we plan to do together as a family?

End with a time for each person to share a thing or two for which they are especially thankful to God. Remind everyone about the dates and times for the next two family dates. Tell them that the second date will be getting into the faith and values of your family, the inner things that you all consider important.

The Second Date: We Believe . . .

Have the tagboard sheets from the first family date on display, light the covenant candle, then share Good Thing/Bad Thing. (See the preceding section on the first date if you need to be refreshed on this beginning.)

Again, hand out magazines and scissors, asking each person to find pictures, words, and phrases in the magazines that say something about who God is and what God does. After everyone has cut out a handful of such items, have each one share what they mean to them as they are glued or taped to a sheet of tagboard (a different color from the last date, if you wish) that has "We Believe in God" written at the top.

Now write on top of the other sheet of tagboard, "People We Admire"; then take turns naming people outside of the immediate family each of you has admired and explain why. (The scribe takes notes.) If too many answers describe people physically, try to steer the conversation around to qualities of a person's character and faith. Brief stories about these people that illustrate the admired qualities would go well here.

Again, with the scribe taking notes, share some of the family stories that illustrate what your family's inner qualities are. A nice balance of both serious and humorous stories would be great. Start with the younger members, if possible; it might be hard for young ones to share stories that they feel compare favorably with the stories of the older family members. On the other hand, they might be the liveliest and most interesting storytellers of all!

Close with a discussion about the following questions:

• What does our magazine montage say about our individual and family faith in God?

• What stories of faith are important to the family? (You might wish to include anecdotes from an earlier generation.)

• What few words might outsiders use to describe what our family values? (Don't discourage critical comments; receive them as of value, like the complimentary comments.)

• Based on the list of names of people we admire, what would you say we value in others? Are some of those qualities in members of our own family?

• How does our family show love? Courage? Anger?

• How might we handle conflict in helpful ways?

End the hour by making a positive comment about the person on your right. Say something like, "I thank God for _____ because. . . ." Remind everyone about the date and time of the next family date. The focus will be on the family's agreeing to make certain promises to each other. Between now and the next date, each person is to write out a single sentence naming something he or she admires about each of the other members of the family ("I thank God for _____ because . . ."). Bring it to the third date and be ready to share your comments about others. If anyone would like help with this assignment, now is the time to ask one other person to help complete the assignment.

The Third Date: We Covenant . . .

Have the tagboard sheets from the preceding two dates displayed in the meeting room. Light the covenant candle and, if you're willing to do so, remind others that this candle will be lit at a meal every day to remind the family about the promises you will make to each other. When the candle is mostly used up, that will signal a time for the family to review the notes and montages from the family covenant, celebrate what has gone well with the promises, and change what needs to be changed. Share Good Thing/Bad Thing, if you like.

Taking notes on another piece of tagboard—with "We Covenant" printed at the top—take turns sharing stories about a promise you kept and felt good about, or a promise someone kept to you.

Then discuss the following questions:

• Can we each think of stories of mutual promises people kept to each other?

• What are some of the spoken or unspoken promises that we each feel certain people commonly make (e.g., the president, a businessperson in your area, fathers and mothers of newborn children, children of aging parents)?

• Does God need our promises before God accepts us? (Look up Ephesians 2:8-9; Romans 5:6-8; 2 Corinthians 12:8-10.)

• Do we have spoken or unspoken promises that bind our family together? What are they? (Take careful notes here.

Examples might include "being there for each other to cele-brate and comfort"; "basic needs will be met"; "I will always love you"; and "you don't have to earn my respect.")

• Take another look at what has been discussed in our three family dates so far. Based on what we see, and what we've dis-cussed, what are the promises that are already active between members of this family? (Focus especially on the way your family makes use of time. Take a moment to affirm each answer. Examples might include: "This family takes time for each other even when we're busy"; "this family takes time for a relationship with God"; and "this family takes weekly time for our church family.")

• Is there anything we can do to make these promises even better and stronger? (In other words, once you affirm strengths, take time next to enhance those strengths.)

• Now, are there family promises that we can add that would make us stronger?

• Are there any promises that we've listed that anyone feels doesn't belong there? (Adjust as needed; it's important for there to be a consensus that the promises listed are worth-while and agreed upon.)

• Can we agree on the promises that remain? (Seek an affir-mation by all members or make changes until you are able to do so.)

Finally, ask each family member, "Do you promise to the rest of the family that you will try to keep the covenant this family has created, to the best of your ability, relying on God's help to do so?"

If you all did the work well with these questions, each person should respond, "I do." If anyone is hesitant to agree, rework the promises of the family covenant until everyone accepts them. If someone still refuses to agree, it doesn't have to ruin the experience. You might comment that sometimes promises are made and kept in one's heart, and it is hoped that each person will take the family promises to heart.

End by pointing out that the entire Bible is a history of people failing in their promises to God and to each other—because of sin—but God is always faithful and does what is needed to bring those people back to the covenant. God will help this family, too! (Read Philippians 1:6; Hebrews 13:5; 6:17-19.)

Close with the Lord's Prayer; hold hands while praying, if possible. Then ask if anyone wants to add any other prayers to this final prayer. Encourage family members to use their homework assignment for the third family date to express why they thank God for each person in the family.

Put the tagboard sheets in a safe place and remember to keep lighting the candle at mealtime (once a day will do). If you care to do so, share Good Thing/Bad Thing at the meals when the candle is lit. When the candle has burned down, retire it with honor and schedule a time to review the family covenant. Start a new candle, and continue with your promises to each other under God's grace and in God's love. You can be certain that God will invite your family back into the covenant as needed.

Chapter 6

Determine What's Worth Our Time

How do we determine the worth of an act? By the money it will make us? By the people it will influence? By how much time off it buys us? By the benefits to self, family, the church? What determines the worthiness of any of our actions?

These are important questions and worth a time-out just to consider them. Time crunches us when we feel we are spending it in less than worthy ways. An urgent action pushes its way past our well-planned schedules and causes, at the very least, inconvenience and heightened amounts of anxiety and fatigue.

Why do we succumb to this barrage of calendar-cluttering activity when we sense underneath that it isn't what's best for our family? When we know that our best times occur when we get away together, relax, and enjoy ourselves and one another? Why are we ourselves often part of the problem, developing workshops, planning meetings, and lengthening kids' sports seasons, all the while complaining about our family's pace of life? Why? Because we bought into the common mentality that the healthier the family, the more involved it is.

It is not uncommon for a "have-to-do-it-right-now" demand to squeeze out a more valuable and worthy activity.

It happens all the time. We've all experienced sitting down to dinner only to have the phone ring and someone is called away. Blessed are those who let the phone ring or shut off the ringers, at least during meals. We can spend a whole life meeting the demands of the moment and never get to the really important stuff.

Having declared loudly that family is important to us and that we intend to do something about it (chapter 1), having taken time to ask some important questions about who we are and what our highest priorities are (chapter 2), having identified some of the areas out of sync with our family's value system (chapter 3), and having repented where needed (chapter 4), having done all the headwork, it now comes down to heart. If you've followed the family covenant process in chapter 5, you've done a lot of important groundwork for what follows. You are better able to answer the questions: What is precious to us? What keeps the whole thing together?

It is the connectedness between ourselves and others and ultimately with God that keeps us from the chaos of self-absorption and creates for us a supportive environment in which we are here for one another. But connectedness takes time and effort.

It's not a simple task. Mary Pipher, author of *The Shelter of Each Other: Rebuilding Our Families,* says it plainly: "Building families . . . involves putting family first, something that is rarely convenient and not always pleasant."[1]

Putting families first means that family health and wholeness becomes our first priority. We determine what's important by returning to the family covenant and asking ourselves some reflective questions to determine the worth of an activity or event:

• Does this activity allow me to keep the family covenant?

• Is this an activity that could be done at another time in life?

- What would be sacrificed in order to say yes to this activity?
- What would be gained?

Using your family covenant as a touchstone to determine what's important allows you to make room for the experiences and activities that keep you connected to God and to family. The covenant acts as a rock, a sure foundation, a wise place on which to build your house as you consider what's worth your time and what's not.

Kennon Callahan, a best-selling author and church consultant, travels the country assisting congregations to identify and build on their strengths first and then gently identify areas where they can develop new strengths. He is a dynamic person who has adapted his credo not only into congregations but into all aspects of his life: job, family, self, friends. His concepts encourage those who listen to say, "Yes, we have an area that needs work, but look how well we're doing over here!" It is an approach that builds on strengths rather than weaknesses and helps encourage a congregation—or a family—to work to make a good thing better.

When looking to determine the worth of an event or activity, let's first begin by looking at places where we already connect. Using the Callahan format, let's think about the people and events we've already deemed "of worth" because of the amount of time we give to them.

Put in the "Big Rocks"

In our first book on lifestyles, *'Tis a Gift to Be Simple: Embracing the Freedom of Living with Less,* we quoted a time manager for business as saying, "The main thing is to keep the main thing the main thing."[2] It's still true. Our time is limited, but the demands on our time seem limitless. It's easy to commit our time to this surplus of demands, lose track of the "main thing," and find ourselves overdrawing our time banks. Without some intentional time budgeting, we run risks similar to when we overspend other resources. And, like the service charges banks tack on for overdrawn accounts, overdrawing time resources will cost people one way or another.

A good children's sermon often speaks to the hearts of a lot of grown-ups too. We once saw a pastor engage his young parishioners with a basketful of odds and ends and a bucket of sand. His goal was to get all the sand and all the gadgets into a large plastic container he had placed on a table. He slowly poured the countless small particles of sand into the container. The sand took up almost half of the space. He then began to add specific items that represented different aspects of a person's life.

"You need time to eat," he stated, throwing in an apple.

"And sleep," a young one piped up, noticing a small doll bed in the pile of items that had not yet been put into the container.

"And time to play, and go to school, and do your home-work," the pastor added, tossing more into the now-crowded container.

"And then there are piano lessons . . . and visits to Grandma and Grandpa . . . and car time . . . and your favorite TV shows."

The point was clear: too many gadgets, not enough space.

The pastor held up a small, white Bible. "How's God going to fit into a life like that?" he asked.

They looked at the overflowing container. Silence.

"Let's try again," the pastor said; he removed the items and dumped the sand back into its original bucket. "Let's put in the things that are really important first."

In went the small Bible, the apple, the doll bed, a picture of a family, and, after some discussion, a TV channel changer. Other important items followed until all the items were in the plastic container.

"Now let's see about the little things!" he said.

He slowly poured the sand back into the container and . . . it all fit.

A simple experiment with a simple point. Putting in the "big rocks," the most important items, first and allowing all the little demands to fit around them assures us that our first priorities, our really important people, don't get shortchanged. If family is a "big rock," then we need to schedule intentional family time before the little things crowd it out. It may mean that some of the sand doesn't get into the container, but we will have met our first objective. The rest can wait.

Jesus modeled this well for us. In an upper room, under a tree, on a mountainside, on the shores of a sea, he gathered his disciples. It was intentional time alone with them. He could have been out preaching to the masses or healing the sick. Instead, he chose to create a space for his disciples, laugh with them, listen to them, encourage them—intentional time that created a relationship that took them through the hard situations when they came.

As a pastor, David could spend all his time meeting the needs of his parish and not those of his family. Many people in other "people-serving" jobs have the same problem. There are reasons why Saint Paul suggests that "ministers" remain single: it takes a tremendous amount of intentionality to meet the needs of family and the needs of others; sometimes, families have to bend.

The trick is to keep families (and complaining spouses) flexible by creating spaces—unmovable spaces—that are all theirs. We like to think of them as "upper-room" moments. Others think of intentional family time as making a deposit of time into the family time account. Banking family time helps families understand and bend when emergencies come up.

Making timely deposits in a family account is as important as depositing your paycheck in the bank. Banking minutes helps the family to manage when somebody or something needs to borrow time from those who not only care for us but care for others. Have you been to the bank lately?

Connecting Points

• When circumstances steal time from you and your family, take that time back when things are less demanding. Tell family members that when they feel shortchanged, they should let you know so you can make a plan to pay it back with time to spare. Be extravagant with how you spend your time. Your family will love you for it.

• When business or outside commitments call you away, give your spouse or kids a rain check. Print up a coupon guaranteeing them a specific amount of "you time" to be collected at a later date. Honor your commitment.

Hold Weekly Calendar Meetings

As our children grow, they acquire not only more stuff but more activities. Add to that an entourage of friends, projects, papers to sign, forms to fill out, checks to write, bag lunches, and requests for small loans—and that's only Monday morning! Does this sound familiar? Running a family when everyone is running demands order and organization.

Families need to communicate calendar items, but they also need time to process concerns, brainstorm ideas, and look at the big picture. All of this communicating takes time and cannot be done when someone is rushing to down a glass of orange juice and head out the door.

Planning the family calendar is a "big rock." Ask any businessperson. Communicating with associates, checking calendars, and getting feedback are what make good companies good. Weekly calendar planning sessions allow all members of the family to have input into the week's schedule. This intentional time allows children a glimpse into the working lives of their parents and models good organizational skills. And you can do it in your pajamas.

As a result of researching and reading for this book, we set aside part of Sunday evening as a time to talk through the week, put big events on the calendar, and check in on everybody. We encourage you to consider doing the same, but be prepared for some balking.

"What did we do wrong?" was the first response we got from all three of our kids when we announced that there would be a family meeting that night in the living room.

"Nothing," we answered, smiling slightly at their uneasiness with this new idea Mom and Dad were laying on them.

"I can't," our oldest began. "Emily is calling and we have to . . ."

"Emily can wait."

So, there they sat, still not convinced that this wasn't going to be about some resurrected misbehavior or failure on their part to follow through on a specific responsibility.

"OK!" I said. "Let's talk about the mornings. It seems that we're having trouble with showers."

"Kate waits until she hears me get up and then she runs into the bathroom and starts running the tub so I can't take a shower with hot water."

"Just wait. This isn't about who's doing what to whom. This is about planning."

The phone rings and Kate jumps up. "It's Em!"

"Ask her to call back."

As with anything new, it's good to set some ground rules at the outset about tattling, finger pointing, and responding to phone calls. Old habits die hard.

And so it began. The shower dilemma was resolved. A specific time for breakfast was established (7:15 A.M. sharp), and times when cars would be leaving was announced. Everyone shared what events they had going for the week, and after the meeting our youngest wrote them on a dry-erase board taped to the refrigerator. They all looked a little shell-shocked when it was over. They were even more amazed when the plan went into action the next morning.

"That's great for today!" Reed said warily. "But it will never last."

I'm happy to report that it is working—most mornings. We leave less frantic, having spent family time eating a meal together and working through the details of the day. Papers are signed at breakfast and checks written. Anxieties about an upcoming test are shared by all and prayers are said. Some come to the table with wet hair, but all have gotten their shower. Other issues have been resolved and the kids have learned the art of compromise and better organization. These are changes for the better that would never have happened if we hadn't taken time to talk, listen, and plan for the week.

Family meetings allow families to share in one another's lives, support one another, and give direction when needed. It's a "big rock," a time-out that keeps us anchored and secure.

"Are we going to meet like this every week?" our youngest asked as he headed to bed.

"Yes. Every Sunday night after supper. Is that OK?"

"I guess. But I bet it doesn't last."

No one's missed a meeting yet.

Create Zones

We had heard the story a hundred times. Jesus, surrounded by a multitude of people, all wanting something from him, stopped and made a space for one woman who had touched his garment. The pastor retold this account using large, sweeping hand gestures, emphasizing the physicalness of the space. It was palpable. Jesus and the woman. A shared space. A murmuring crowd, made, perhaps, more silent by the moment. Such personal attention would make a person feel very special.

Robert Morgan, a Baptist minister and author of an article titled "Life in the Blender," encourages families—and especially fathers—to carve out spaces for their wives and children, to create zones where parent and child or husband and wife can share a space, reconnect, and make each other feel special.[3]

Morgan and his wife eat breakfast together Saturdays and Mondays at a local restaurant where they compare schedules and share a few moments of uninterrupted time. It doesn't just happen; they plan it that way. They also plan time for each child to spend a weekly one-on-one with their dad. Morgan writes, "Typically, I take one child to breakfast before school on Wednesday or Thursday. I'll pick up another after school for ice cream. I'll plan a date with the third. And Fridays and Saturdays are set aside as a sort of 'sabbath' in which, even if I study, I do it at home with an 'interrupt me' attitude."[4]

A growing number of busy parents are creating zones in which they set aside space for children and for each other. A long-running commercial, for example, portrayed a busy mother fielding calls from clients at home as her two young daughters looked on. Somewhere between rings, one little girl piped up, "When can I be a client?" The repentant mother gathered up girls, sun umbrellas, and beach paraphernalia and headed for the local sand dunes, mobile phone in hand.

If we fail to provide zones for family interaction, children will find their own zones. Zoning out in front of the TV has become the activity of choice for American children. Even back in 1989, "the average child in the United States still spent more time watching television than any other activity except sleeping," according to the American Academy of Pediatrics.[5]

If that's not enough to make parents stop and think, Dr. James Twitchell, author of *The Carnival Culture*, reports that by age six, an American child "will have invested more hours watching television than in speaking with his or her father over an entire lifetime."[6]

The point here is not to bemoan the evils of TV (discussed in chapter 3). The point is attitude. Morgan writes about an "interrupt me" attitude when he takes work home. It's an attitude shared by a lot of parents who care about their parenting. Tiger Woods's dad made that point in an interview when he said that he always took time to answer his son's questions. To him, his son was his first job; anything else was second.

It's a madding crowd we live in. Lots of people make demands on us. Lord, help us to be the kind of parents who, when someone big or little tugs on our garments, we stop and create a space for them. The crowds can wait.

Connecting Points

• Consider following Morgan's example and create specific times for each child to have one-on-ones with each parent.

• Car rides create a zone of their own. Take one child along when you go to the grocery store or run an errand. Some of the most meaningful discussions with our kids can be on these short jaunts.

• If you have younger children, spend a night building a fort. Kids love enclosed spaces. (Tents have the same effect.) Plan a picnic on the floor.

• Create a zone in your home where people can go if they need private space. One mother of eight turned a corner chair toward the wall when she needed space. When she was in the chair, she was not available to her children unless there was an emergency.

• Continue to protect the zones you have already established: mealtime, prayers before meals and bedtime, bedtime routines.

- Create a family posture when having a family discussion (e.g., knees touching or everyone on their stomachs). Creating a physical zone keeps everyone focused and literally connected to one another.

The Greatest of These Is Love

David is fond of saying, "There are two kinds of love: need love and gift love." It's easy to sense the difference. The former is given in order to get; the latter is given with nothing required in return. Let that thought sink in. Think of a person who gave you gift love. Think again of a time when someone asked for love from you. Which kind of love, need love or gift love, comes more easily from you? Love is a "big rock." Some would say it's the only rock that is really worth our time.

Need love and gift love flow freely back and forth among members as we "family" one another. It gives us stability and a commitment to one another. A commitment to family helps to order all the other rocks in our lives.

What kind of face does this type of commitment wear? According to David Anderson, project director for the Augsburg Youth and Family Institute at Augsburg College in Minneapolis, "Commitment to the family involves prioritizing how individual members are using their time, dropping less important agendas, and adjusting schedules to include the family."[7] That is gift love.

Our family "crunches" or gets "time-trapped" just like other families with whom we've talked. Some days we swim with the current. Other days we cling to rocks. Some days we lie exhausted on the beach. Making family takes work and time.

If you've been parenting for a while, you have faced the turbulent, tentative years when your young, clinging ones now want out of the nest. These are the tension-release years, when you try to keep your hands on the reins without them knowing it, trying to let them think they "have the power," giving them choices as the budding pre-adult starts to push off.

But at the very time they're telling us they don't need us, they are also sending messages that they don't really mean it. It's need love at its most precious. And, for a few years more, it is gift love from us.

Recently, I (Barbara) found myself looking at preholiday commitments I had made: concerts, rehearsals, getting people on board. With this book deadline approaching and conferences and grades to contend with at work, I was over-booked. It showed at home: laundry piled up; bills sat unsent; laughter appeared only on occasion. I complained that I needed more help. It came, but not without a fight: "I'm a kid. I shouldn't have to grocery shop. . . ."

It took me four hours of cooling off before I heard the rest of that sentence. "I shouldn't have to grocery shop . . . without you." I'm glad I took time to listen for the unspoken part of that sentence. It made all the difference as we approached the Christmas season.

As a result, the community Christmas concert happened under new leadership. Instead, I made bread with my young girl-women, and we delivered the loaves to surprised friends. We laughed in the car. We moved into Advent with time to prepare. We did not slap this Christmas together. We felt comforted, not hammered, by David Anderson's patient and kind words: "Commitment to the family involves prioritizing how individual members are using their time, dropping less important agendas, and adjusting schedules to include the family."[8]

Connecting Points

• Ask family members what they would want to do if they could have one evening free to be with the family. Don't be quick to jump in with ideas. Allow for thinking time. Make plans to grant each other's wishes.

• Plan an afternoon or evening with no expectations. In our overscheduled society, it's a foreign idea to not have anything to do. Stay with it until it feels comfortable to you. Listen as the laughter returns to your conversations.

• Take another look at your responses to the Family Time Trap Survey (chapter 2) and your family covenant (chapter 5). Make adjustments to family schedules that reflect your commitment to family.

• Practice giving and receiving "gift love." Give value to those activities that require a high love price tag. Encourage each other when you see deeds done in love. Point out to smaller children when these acts occur.

Chapter 7

Reclaim Rituals,
Make Memories,
Strengthen the Connection

We asked our daughter Kate if she thought our family had any rituals. After some thought, she said she couldn't think of any. At first, our defense mechanisms kicked in. We suggested that of course we had family rituals and rattled off a list of "suggestions" for her to consider.

Her response made us pause and give thanks. "Oh, that. Aren't those things that we just sort of do? They aren't rituals, are they?"

In his book *The Twelve Days of Christmas*, Harold Belgum reflects on the topic of family ritual: "Family rituals are events that involve the whole family and are carried out in a certain way at a certain time. There is a general feeling that they are good things to do and that there is a right way for our family to do them. They bring a blessing."[1] Belgum is convinced of the impact of such rituals on families: "Christian family rituals are of profound importance in the character formation of children. They help to develop Christian attitudes, values and habits that will control their lives as they grow and have their own families. Family rituals have a way of relating young and old—of weaving the family together. Strong families like rituals. Rituals help make strong families."[2]

Think about the way your family celebrates special days such as Christmas, Thanksgiving, and Easter. Consider the rituals that surround birthdays, baptisms, and first communions. Don't forget the little acts incorporated into bedtime routines, Saturday mornings, or evening snacks. Take a moment to give thanks for the connectedness these celebrations bring to your family and those you love. Remember these rituals and keep them holy. These are the times families connect. These are the moments that help define who we are.

Rituals of Identity

For Kate to say that our family had no rituals really meant that the many repeated actions done on her behalf had become so embedded—so much a part of herself—that they simply were. They were daily gifts of love freely given, grace. What are some of the common quiet rituals found in your family? Do you always eat pancakes on Saturday morning? Do you always take a certain street home just because it goes by the river? It's the always moments, and the always people, that create for us a sense of stability. Sometimes it is the small, seemingly insignificant, recurring actions that in the end connect us to our true identity as a family.

Our family moved to Long Prairie, Minnesota, at Christmas. David preached his first sermon at American Lutheran Church on Christmas Eve. After the service, we loaded the kids into the car and headed three hours south to Mankato and our extended family. We remembered to pack clothes for church, to bring the presents, to fill the car with gas—but forgot that almost nothing is open on Christmas Eve. We stopped at a convenience station and bought dried-out sandwiches, a carton of chocolate milk, and, for dessert, malted milk balls. We got lost on a foggy gravel road and arrived late. Sleepy relatives welcomed us. In many ways, it is our most memorable Christmas.

As much as we love creating memories, and enjoy having those memories come back year after year, it is not the doing but the being that creates the family identity. Ritual requires relationship, a connectedness to those we love and have loved. Christmas may not be the same without the twinkling lights and the familiar dinner, but it would still be Christmas. It is not the trimmings that give us identity, but the joined worship that moves us past tradition onto more holy ground.

It is not the pancakes we eat on a Saturday morning but with whom we eat them. Ritual is not so much taking the same scenic ride home at the end of a busy day as it is who rides with us to share the beauty and who waits for us at home to hear about our day. In a sense we are, in the end, made up of the people we have loved and the people who have loved us.

Bedtime prayers make brief, simple, daily rituals. Other rituals are passed along once a year or once a generation. They speak of shared interest and a sense of the significant. Creating and celebrating our rituals with others, in whatever form they may come, is a high priority for families who want to work at being family.

Connecting Points

• Looking back on your family covenant, what family rituals from your past have become a legacy in your family? What rituals helped shape your family covenant? How does what we do tell us who we are?

• Invite several families and friends over for an evening. Take informal family pictures for one another. If you have a camera with a timer, try to get a group shot. Share the prints. Place them in a prominent spot and be thankful for people who share our rituals and who help create a sense of family for us.

Rituals of Affection

Our daughter Jill picked up a book we had purchased, *Wonderful Ways to Love a Teen . . . Even When It Seems Impossible* by Judy Ford.[3] Being halfway through her fifteenth year, Jill was greatly offended. Even with all the bad press given teenagers and what could be considered good-natured complaining done by parents, Jill has never considered herself "impossible" to love. She has no reason to believe that she is anything other than God's wonderful girl who occasionally messes up and is forgiven.

Since she was born, we have told her daily that she is loved. We whisper it at night before bed, we yell it out the car window when we drop her off to school, we repeat it when she is facing a difficult task. We remind her when she is angry with us that we love her. Saying "I love you" to Jill and our other children has become a daily ritual for us. It is a ritual that was passed down to us from our own families.

When David was stationed in Thailand during the Vietnam War, he would on occasion attempt to make a ham radio connection to phone home. It was a cumbersome process involving people at several stations spanning twelve time zones who would repeatedly switch from transmit to receive simultaneously in order to allow the conversation to take place. Toward the end of one conversation, his mother's voice began to break up.

"I can't hear you! Over!" he shouted into the mike.

Across the miles, the radio operators dutifully switched over in order for his mother to try again, but he heard only static and a few unintelligible sounds.

"I can't hear you! Over!" he tried again.

Again, there was static. Suddenly, a gruff, male voice interrupted the noise with a simple sentence.

"She says she loves you! Over."

A family ritual, breaking through the chaos, to give encouragement and bring connectedness to one so far away.

Children or spouses don't have to go halfway around the world to have communication become distorted or break down altogether. It can happen in our living rooms or across a dinner table. Sometimes it's followed by a slammed door, a gunned engine, an empty place. Time stands still then, and we would wish for a few familiar rituals.

Rituals become a welcome part of our lives, all the more often if we have prepared for them, using a well-grooved phrase, etched in our hearts by repetition. "I love you" rolls out of our hearts and off of our tongues and across the static to be interpreted not by a gruff, male voice but by a bent body broken in love, a voice crying out from a cross, saying, "God says he loves you! Over!" Even when the door is slammed, the engine gunned, the place at the table empty, we are not alone. We are still and will always be connected to a God who loves us.

The "I love you" ritual can come in many languages. An article in *McCall's* listed twenty-five ways to say "I love you" that included foot rubs, nicknames, and being silly.[4] Judy Ford's book, *Wonderful Ways to Love a Teen . . .* , despite a title some might find offensive, contains many methods for saying "I love you," such as allowing privacy, admitting when you're wrong, and teaching your children to pray.

How well Jesus modeled this ritual of loving, finding hundreds of ways to say "I love you" to those who needed to hear it! Time-honored rituals help us to escape from the family time trap by building holy moments into our days and lives. Well-grooved rituals encourage us to enter our home, take off our shoes, and declare this a holy place.

Connecting Points

• Ask your family members if you have any family rituals. Help them to see "rituals" in the small things.

• Discuss how everyday rituals help "make family."

• Make your own top-ten list of ways to say "I love you" to members of your family, or brainstorm with family members ten ways your family already says "I love you" to one another. Write them down and hang them on the refrigerator.

Rituals of Faith

Rituals that take a sacred form happen, in a sense, outside of time, within a bigger time frame than the twenty-four-hour one in which we're used to running. We sense something eternal in our rituals of faith, something that reminds us that God has been, is, and will be faithful, something that connects us to those who have come before us and to those who will join us in the future.

This larger-than-life concept of time became clearer as we prepared for our second daughter's confirmation, having just buried our great-grandmother, GiGi. We framed GiGi's confirmation certificate for Jill. She will remember singing "Great Is Thy Faithfulness" at GiGi's funeral. Jill will know that the God who is her God was faithful to GiGi all her life. In one sense, GiGi's death represents a passing of the baton, a ritual of faith that connects one generation to another. Now it is Jill's turn to run the good race. God willing, Jill will share the faith with her own child someday and we will prepare for a confirmation once again. A faithful God from generation to generation.

The church is listening to the needs of families as they struggle to make faith connections. And they need encouragement. In the Lutheran denomination alone, there has been a 10-percent decrease in infant baptisms since 1990. This comes at a time when "we're experiencing a second baby boom unlike anything since the 1950s," according to David Anderson. Anderson encourages families to "make use of mealtime, bedtime, lap time, car time, and sick-day time" to nurture faith in the family.[5]

But a lot of us need help in this area. In a sense, churches have taken over the role of family in creating faith rituals. Parents may rely too heavily on Sunday school teachers and pastors to pass on the stories of faith. It is important that children hear from our own lips our own faith stories—stories of our baptism, confirmation, prayers answered, and doubts we've dealt with. Teach your children to pray and to listen as you pray. Let them catch you reading your Bible. Sit together during worship.

Anderson identifies four "keys" for practical faith nurturing: "caring conversations, family devotions, family service projects among two or more generations, and family rituals."[6] Take time to think about how your family might develop faith opportunities in these four areas.

Rituals of faith develop not so much from what we do or say as from remembering whose we are, who claims us, who names us, who shows us what it means to be loved, and who would give their life for us if necessary. Rituals provide a unique kind of communion, a bringing together into one body, where we do in order to remember.

Connecting Points

• Make a list of faith rituals already present in your family. Share a prayer of thanksgiving for each one. Light a candle with each prayer. You will be blessed by a room full of light.

• Create a family banner by "stamping" the hand of each family member on a plain-colored piece of cotton cut and hemmed to form a table runner. Poster or fabric paint works well for this. Add your own special touches to make it your own. Use it for family devotions.

Making Memories from Moments

In an warmhearted article titled "Something Wonderful This Way Comes," Clark Cothern shares a "making time" moment he had with his six-year-old son as they camped out in the loft of their garage. Not exactly Yosemite, Cothern admitted, but not without its own unique adventure. Cothern writes, "My son and I were braving the elements together—splinters, spiders, gas fumes, hungry animals" (a nocturnal visit from a friendly raccoon). Cothern called this nighttime adventure a "rite of passage," remembering a cold night with his own father thirty-one years in the past.[7]

Making time for adventure creates its own ripple effect. It would not be surprising if thirty years hence Cothern's son wrote an article detailing a similar adventure he shared with his own son—third-generation memories, rituals in the making. We appreciate such memories only when we're old enough to know that it's our turn to pass on the magic to someone else.

Although some adventures can be planned, others appear out of the blue: all we need do is grab hold and run with them. Our oldest child was just five when a beautiful double rainbow appeared in our backyard. Five-year-olds are really into rainbows: they draw them, paint them, and sticker them on just about everything. Calling to our two girls to "come see," David pointed out the kitchen window. Their jaws dropped. There was a luscious double rainbow against a satiny, black sky.

"Hey," the five-year-old said without a hint of disbelief, "there's a pot of gold at the end of the rainbow, and it looks like it ends just over there by Hilmar and Alice's house!" The three-year-old's eyes glistened as if it were Christmas Eve. Sensing a serendipitous moment, we bundled them into the car and chased the rainbow for the pot of gold.

Our oldest, noticing cars coming up behind us, bounced up and down and urged, "Hurry up, Daddy, they're after the gold!" He smiled and pressed a little heavier on the gas pedal.

When we reached Hilmar and Alice's house, the rainbow had moved to the next ridge. Then it moved to an open field two miles further east, and so on. Before we could reach the elusive pot of gold, the rainbow had dissipated with the setting sun.

On the way home, the girls were quiet. Then, from the backseat we heard a quiet and reflective voice: "Dad, I think I know what happened. God moved the rainbow because we wanted the gold too much." We had a thoughtful discussion about "wanting" on the way home. We didn't have gold coins to show, but we had certainly found our treasure in a family adventure that afternoon.

Whether we discover adventure in the loft of garages or find it chasing rainbows, we need to give thanks for it, claim it, and proclaim it worthy of our time. Making time for adventure is rarely wasted.

It's often in the foolish moments, the times when we grab the moment and run, that we discover the most meaning, laughter, and connectedness. Saint Paul felt something similar in 1 Corinthians 4:10 when he talked about being a "fool for Christ." Rituals of adventure remind the grown-up in us that we create the environment for our children. Children march to our drum so often; it is a wise person who makes time to march to theirs. Who knows, in doing so you might find your own pot of gold.

Connecting Points

• Spend time tonight with your family and enjoy a favorite family snack. While you eat, play "Remember when. . . ." Retell favorite memories: times when you made time for adventure, grabbed a moment and took off, created something beautiful for the family. Remember rituals of adventure.

• Put your family into the car but don't tell them where you are going. On your way, have fun guessing the destination.

Whether you end up at the zoo, the beach, or the ice cream parlor, you'll have one more adventure to share.

Rituals of Routine

Although it is impossible to create more time, we can create more moments. Most of our day ticks off unnoticed, but it is the moments that we do notice for which we live. Some call this "mindfulness"—those split seconds that stretch into memory: a hand held; a beautiful sunset; a look in someone's eye; a moment of quiet.

Mindfulness doesn't create more time, but it allows us to enjoy the time we have. One such moment came when we had just spent the summer working on our oldest daughter's bedroom. Because of newfound allergies, we tore up her carpet, only to discover a beautiful maple floor underneath, much in need of repair. With the confidence of novices, we bought stripper, stain, and polyurethane and rolled up our sleeves. Two months later we were still at work repairing it.

The day finally came when Kate could move back into her room. Kate, Grandma Joyce, and I (Barbara) all stood in the room together. Sensing the connectedness of three generations of women, I grabbed their hands and said, "We're so lucky!" We stood for a few silent seconds, holding hands. "We're having a Kodak moment!" Kate exclaimed, and we all laughed.

Parents and active kids often live in a fragmented time frame. It's worth the energy, however, to try to bring the whirling daily activities and scattered thinking into the here and now. Live in the present. Creating time, in the form of mindfulness, requires little time and little money. What it does require is practice and the willingness of at least one family member to notice the moment it happens and to draw the attention of the others to it.

Mary Pipher, author of *The Shelter of Each Other: Rebuilding Our Families,* suggests two ways that families can connect with mindfulness—one through work and one through routine. Shared work allows time for conversation, develops a sense of interdependence, and allows for a variety of learning.

I (David) learned to sing harmony while doing dishes with my mother after supper. Many of these spontaneous evening recitals are stored in my memory and sometimes I regrets the convenience of our dishwasher, which takes only a few minutes to load. Machines bought to save us time sometimes rob us of our time together.

"Routine protects time," according to Pipher. Routine, even though we often buck it, acts as a comfort blanket when activities get unmanageable. It gives families and children a sense of control. Our son, Reed, on his first night at Bible camp, said that at first he was afraid. But then he remembered that at home we always end the day by saying, "Don't forget to thank God for something." And so, in the darkness of his cabin, he thanked God and found comfort in the familiar ritual casually repeated as we closed the door to his room each night.

Shared work and routine are two ways to create more time. Author Dolores Curran would add another—rules. In her book *Stress and the Healthy Family,* she lists several rules shared with her by children who live in what she terms "stress-effective" families:[8]

- Make your bed when you get up.
- Put your clothes in the hamper or they don't get washed.
- Empty the dishwasher before you go to school.
- Feed the dog before you eat breakfast.
- Come in the first time you're called.
- Do the dishes after dinner while Mom and Dad take a walk.

Some would call these rules "work." If done all or most of the time, they become routine. Curran states that "in families with no specific rules (and we could add here families with no 'routine' or 'shared work') parents are often run ragged by inspections, pleading and refighting daily issues and eventually give up. . . . It's easier to do it myself."[9] It sounds so familiar. How many wheels do we have to invent before we quit running?

Creating time through shared work and routine, whether in the form of rules or not, buys families together time. If, by creating routine, sharing responsibility, and establishing rules for the family, we can recover lost time, we have in a sense created time and a chance to become mindful.

Connecting Points

• At a family meeting, have each person share with the others one big improvement they would like to see in the family. Then discuss it as a family. Encourage a sense of mutuality and responsibility, asking family members often, "Are you able to contribute to this improvement?"

• Take twenty minutes after an evening meal or before bed to do a quick sweep of the house. Everyone helps. Set a timer to give it a sense of urgency. When the timer goes off, meet for a snack. Discuss why shared work can be fun.

* * * * *

If you are a main caretaker of the home front, consider leaving little reminder notes to family members who are making work for you. With older kids, a cute note reading "Please Clear Off This Counter When You're Finished" works better than a face-to-face confrontation. Notes can be placed on lights, dresser mirrors, or pillows. You might find response notes on your pillow at night.

Chapter 8

Take Time Out

For a tired and stressed-out family, time-outs can work a regenerating miracle. Pack up your family for a week-long retreat, a day out of town, or even five minutes of back rubs. These "sabbaths" and "mini-sabbaths" allow all family members the time to rest, recuperate, and return refreshed and with a new perspective.

How many times did Jesus take his twelve disciples to the sea, a mountain, a garden, or an upper room? How many times did he gather two or three around him for a quiet day away from the ministry? How many times did he lay his hands on an individual and create a time-out space for some-one who needed his attention? Give your family the gift of a time-out in whatever form it might take. Treat those moments as holy, as gifts of sabbath, as time away to focus on what's really important: one another.

The All-Important Family Vacation

We lay inside our five-person tent, our bodies huddled together around a Coleman lantern. Jill laid down a seven of clubs and we all groaned loudly. She had all the clubs. There was nothing to do but slough.

Sensing defeat, Reed stuck his flashlight inside his mouth and turned on the light. His face glowed in the dark. Two more flashlights came out and two more faces, illumined from the inside, glowed eerily at the others. All five heads huddled together, three with light coming out of their nostrils and eye sockets. It was, as our oldest noted, "really cool."

Four years after our youngest was born, remembering some of our own family vacation memories as kids, we wanted to create some memories for our own children. Long miles in the car became great family time. We were captive to each other, and despite the occasional argument over who sat where and the unstoppable urge to ask, "Are we there yet?" we loved it. Once, as we traveled on a Sunday, we held a make-shift service in the car. Kate gave an original sermon on the Noah's ark story, Jill led the singing, and Reed tried to collect money from everyone. We all gave thanks.

We've made three large trips since then, as well as many little ones. Each time away has been filled with family-only, one-of-a-kind, had-to-be-there moments. We learned as a family to navigate unfamiliar roads, work our way through a variety of places under construction, be quiet when driving is hard, and sing when the monotony of the miles begins to wear on us. We've shared the awe of the ocean, the insanity of an insect attack, and the excited uneasiness of going through a really long tunnel. And we learned that it's not about the destination; it's about the journey—a good metaphor for raising a family.

Someday, when our kids' lives take them into their own dark tunnels or they have to work their way around other unfamiliar territory, we hope they will make a conscious connection between life and all these "lessons" learned from inside and outside a car. But if they don't do so consciously, it doesn't matter. It's part of their experience, and they'll have it when they need it.

How often we hear people say, "We don't have time for vacations!" Our response is, "You don't have time not to take a vacation." For families, vacations are not luxuries; they are the stuff that the family is made of. Vacations send the message

"I can leave everything behind because all I need is you" to our kids and our spouse. That kind of affirmation creates good soil for young ones to put down roots and grow, good memories to carry into their future, memories that will call to them when they have a family of their own, memories that will drag them out onto the roads with tent in hand, a deck of cards, and the opportunity to do nothing more than be together.

It was not surprising, then, that when David asked a group of sixth-graders what their favorite family memories were, almost all of them said family vacations. As parents, we need to hear that. Our children want to be with us even when they act like they don't. And they need us to want to be with them. Don't say you don't have the time, that the resources aren't there. It isn't *where* you go, it's *that* you go. Take with you only what you really need. Your children will thank you for it.

Connecting Points

• Talk to other families about vacations that worked for them. We once met a couple who had traveled extensively. Their memories of a trip around Lake Superior encouraged us to make the same trip. Most trips involve three things: the anticipation, the traveling, and the remembering. Don't short-change any of these.

• After our last trip, our kids edited our five vacation videos down into one, and added music and some cute titles. (They did this themselves, using one of the many simple editing programs available now.) They presented it to us as a gift. It was interesting to see what they picked out as the important aspects of the trip. Their video ended with a frozen frame of us on board a boat, which was taking us away from the shores of Mackinac Island in Lake Superior, as our hair blew wildly and we looked at each other and laughed. Priceless!

- If money is tight, swap houses with a friend or a family member for a week. Or consider family camps, which often have family rates. Getting out of town for the day offers a much-needed break.

- While on vacation, take turns sharing the photo responsibilities so that everyone gets to take pictures. Don't be shy in asking strangers to take shots of all of you together. Place the best photo on your refrigerator until your next adventure.

- Take out your calendar and mark your vacation days, and treat them as if they were set in stone. Begin making plans.

Worship Together

As a pastor's family, we don't always get the chance to sit together during church. Sometimes when a guest speaker gives the sermon, David comes down and joins us. That is always special—especially during the singing, when we can hear his voice together with ours.

David once worked as an assistant to the bishop of our synod in northwestern Wisconsin. He was on the road like a traveling salesman, touching base with some of the 216 congregations in his area. Rarely would we even see him on a Sunday. The kids and I (Barbara) would go to services and Sunday school together, but we missed him. Reed, then age four, forgot that his dad was a pastor and thought he had become a fireman. If our kids had been older, we could have traveled with him. Worshiping together means that much to us.

Getting everyone up and to church on a Sunday morning can be difficult, especially if you have little ones who need help dressing or reluctant teenagers who never get enough sleep. Sometimes it doesn't seem worth it.

When our kids were small, I would rush from Sunday school into church, dragging bags of distractions for the service: Cheerios, M&Ms, books, color crayons. I felt that I was there but my head wasn't. By the end of the service, I had managed to keep the children fairly quiet, but felt I was personally getting nothing from the service. Still, I was being faithful, and for those years, that was enough.

As I look back on that time, I can see that God was faithful to my faithfulness. Now, as our children ask to sit with friends or sit with the choir, I remember those Sundays with a full heart. I had the opportunity to be with the children for an entire hour, put my arms around them, hold them on my lap, help them find the songs in the hymn book, and hear them mimic the liturgy in their young voices. How excited they would get when they knew parts of the service. "The Lord's Prayer is coming now" I would whisper, and they'd get ready to join in. They'd eagerly wait to put their quarters into the offering plate. These are wonderful, cherished memories.

Worship is a necessary time-out for families. It really matters if you show up on a Sunday morning. Roland Martinson, well known for his work in youth ministry, has written, "The best indicator of whether or not teenagers will be active worshipers and congregational participants is the past and continued participation of their parents in the life of the church."[1] Remembering the Sabbath and keeping it may keep those we love surrounded by a caring community of believers long enough to get them through the difficult years.

In the end, it's not the sermon or music that does it—although it all helps!—it's the fact that we come together, worship together. It's a family thing, and our God is faithful. Worship is a necessary time-out, a "big rock" in the planning of our weekly schedule. Don't miss out on the blessing.

Connecting Points

• Ask your children if they know someone who doesn't have a "church family." Ask them to invite their friends to Sunday school and offer to include them in the morning's plans. Entire families have been renewed and blessed by such a strategy.

- Create a family altar somewhere in your house, or add candles or similar items to the kitchen table to help your family use mealtime in a more devotional way. Think of your mealtime as a type of worship. Begin and end it with prayer. Tell a story. Hold hands. Be the body of Christ united.

Family Fun

We shared a common interest with our friends the Boardmans when it came to family and family ministry. Our social time with them always included topics of mutual interest and we began to collaborate on organizing a weekend retreat that would offer families time to reflect on who they were as families. We created a format that included the Boardmans' interests in art and counseling and ours in music and storytelling. Ideas flew, notebooks filled up, proposals were written. We enjoyed working with them and learned from them. They knew how to balance fun and work.

Just when our focus would begin to wane, Rich would throw down his pencil, grab one of his kids, and say, "Time to take a break!" We'd end up at a swimming beach or at a park, and it was clear that this was not a place to talk shop. Rich knew that fun was as necessary as the work.

If you ever visit a Benedictine center for a few days, you will soon notice a rhythm to their day: work, study, quiet time, and play are all centered around regular times for prayer. It is a structured day that brings balance to both body and soul. The Boardmans may not have known about the Benedictine way of life, but they shared something in common with the fifteen-hundred-year-old Benedictine tradition. They knew that recreation—planned time-outs, spiritual siestas—were as necessary to the healthy family as hard work, study, and worship.

Healthy families need to have fun together. It's a time-crunch issue and a necessary, intentional time-out taken for the sole purpose of enjoying one another. It depends on individual families, but the experts seem to agree that the most happy families are the ones who put work aside and share a minimum of one fun activity a week. This is a doable goal, one worth thinking about.

Connecting Points

• Spend an evening looking at your old family videos or pictures. Tell stories.

• Make thumbprint cookies and deliver them to an unsuspecting neighbor.

• Gather the troops and a ball of your choice (soccer has been ours) and head to the nearest schoolyard. Run yourself crazy.

• Check out the closest bike paths in your state. Hang a state map in a prominent place and highlight all trails you conquer. (This makes for an interesting summer project.)

• Rent a canoe or a boat for the day.

• Teach your kids a card game you can all play together. Invite friends over and make an evening of it.

• As part of your usual schedule, plan a short personal retreat for each day, a significant outing for the family each week, a weightier retreat every month, and a really good getaway vacation every year. Money is not the key here; creativity and togetherness are the only currency that count.

Care for the Caregivers

Bending, I (Barbara) stopped myself halfway down. My friend had already noticed my strange posturing. Straightening myself up, we stood eye to eye. Then, after a few moments of bemused silence: "You were going to tie my shoelaces for me, weren't you?" she stated with a let's-face-the-facts kind of voice.

"Ah . . . no . . . not really," I lied through my teeth.

"Yes, you were. We were talking. You looked at my shoes and then you started to bend down to tie them. Come on. Be honest."

I stared down at my friend's sprawling laces, looked up at her now sprawling smile, and decided on the truth.

"Reflexes," I said.

"You," she stated quite seriously, "have been in the house too much!"

In my defense, I should have stuck with the reflex theory, but I had just answered the phone that morning with "Hello, this is Mama." It was time to ask some of those hard primary-caregiver questions once again. As much as I loved being at home with my kids, I needed some time to myself.

For those who work in and out of the home, the idea of staying home sounds heavenly some days. But there are ditches on both sides of the work-or-stay-home dilemma and both ditches carry their own type of time traps.

The working parent may find the day chopped into fifteen-minute increments neatly displayed in a daily planner, but the stay-at-home parent faces a day that has no beginning and no ending, and little or no predictable plan. Finding time away from "in-house" responsibilities is as necessary as the ten-minute coffee break at work or the one-hour business lunch. These personal time-outs act as mini-sabbaths and bring us back to all those ongoing demands with our shoelaces tied and a needed fresh perspective.

Working parents, on the other hand, often see their off-work hours as family time. It seems selfish to take time away from family when one has been away all day.

Personal time. Family time. There is a fine line between them. We've all walked that line at one time or another, whether we stay home or go out to work. And, being the good caregivers we are, we tend to shortchange ourselves and end up tying our best friend's shoes for her. Even Jesus, as committed as he was, left his "family" and went off at times to be alone, to recenter himself, to remember his calling. His children didn't run off looking for another messiah. They let him have his space.

You know if you're doing good parenting. Let your children tie their own shoes once in a while. In the meantime, go have yourself a little fun. They'll thank you for it.

Connecting Points

• Children don't always understand the need a parent has for personal space. Anyone who has had a two-year-old pounding on the outside of the bathroom door can vouch for this. Tie in your time away with some special treat for your children. Get the baby-sitter the children always ask for. Leave a little something under their pillow. Give them a special object of yours to guard while you're gone. Help them learn early to value time to themselves.

• Think about the difference between being "responsible for" and "responsible to" people who have been placed in your care. How might that difference affect your caregiving of those people?

• Encourage your spouse to take an overnight away from home once a month. Mark your calendar now for the weeks ahead. Pack his or her lunch/suitcase if you wish.

Laughter and
the Five-Minute Time-Out

Leslie Gibson, a home health-care nurse and humor consult-ant, wears a button that reads "Frogs have it easy. They eat what bugs them." When family life becomes rather buggy, when the time crunch moves past the pinching point and really begins to hurt, how can we become more like frogs? How can we learn to "eat" what bugs us? Laugh at it. Then go find a friend and laugh again. By the time the family gets home, you'll be acting more like the prince you really are. Laughter is a cheap and easy time-out that requires no plan-ning ahead, no extra financing, and virtually no time. It's free. What a gift!

Kids do a lot more laughing than adults. The average four-year-old laughs four hundred times a day, the average adult, fifteen.[2] The statistics speak for themselves. Kids can teach adults a lot in this regard.

Much of the time stress parents place on themselves and their kids could be erased with a slight attitude adjustment, experts point out. "Stress is not an event. It's how we view an event," says Joel Goodman, director of the Humor Project in Saratoga Springs, New York.[3] A small time-out to stop and breathe, change our perspective, and see the gift in the situa-tion is good advice.

Here is a case in point: I (Barbara) was really upset with one of our children for not taking her studies seriously. A conference with one of her teachers one morning reinforced the fact that she had been sloughing off. Sadly for our middle one, I work in the same school she attends. I set off in a huff to find her and set things right. Our daughter saw me com-ing down the hall and knew the truth was out. What to do? Where to hide? She opted for humor. Before I could begin to give her a knee-jerk lecture on responsibility, our daughter closed her eyes, made large circles in front of herself with her hands, and repeated, "Bre-e-e-athe . . . bre-e-e-e-athe." It was disarming. After a laugh together, we had our talk.

A five-minute time-out can come in the form of a table prayer sung to a familiar melody such as "The Addams Family." It can reach out and grab a family member and dance them into the next room (no music required). A five-minute time-out can pull a lanky adolescent over your knees for a few minutes of back-scratching. Five-minute time-outs help us lighten the family time crunch or dismiss it altogether. The least it will do is leave a smile on our face. Not bad for five minutes.

Laughter is a gift. When spontaneous laughter disappears or seldom erupts during the course of the day, it is a warning flag. Lighten up. Finding the humor in a situation beats getting mad any day. Have you laughed with your family today?

Connecting Points

• See who can make the silliest laugh. Give awards.

• Rent the video *Mary Poppins* and play the scene with the song "I Love to Laugh."

• Lie on the floor and rest your heads on the stomach of another family member. Take turns saying "ha" hard enough to make the other person's head bounce. Speed the game up. Enjoy!

• The next time you feel like getting mad, try to laugh it off. See what happens.

Chapter 9

"As for Me and My House . . ."

Our oldest was in a rather typical early teen funk where music blared from behind closed doors, her bed went unmade more often than not, and dishes would be cleared only if she was asked—maybe. Too much time was spent in passive activities: watching television, "chatting" on the Internet, or commiserating with friends on the phone. It got to us.

"Where are the passion and idealism and energy that are supposed to accompany the flowering of youth?" we wondered, conveniently forgetting our own journey through those years. "You're off to volunteer at the nursing home," we said, hoping that straw of an idea would result in a changed attitude.

At first, it was just one more thing to remind her to remember. Then, at dinner one night, we shared Good Thing/Bad Thing, as we often do, where each person shares the best thing that happened during the day, or the worst thing, or both.

Kate jumped right in. "After school, I helped an old man at the nursing home put on his socks. Eeeew! You should have seen the gnarled toes. Gross! He really thanked me. A lot. And the bad thing that happened to me was that I didn't do well on my science test."

We wondered if we had heard correctly. The gnarled toes were the highlight of her day? No question about it. In her service to the man with the gross and gnarled toes, she shed a layer of self-centeredness and made a connection with something bigger than herself.

A small miracle manifested by a changed attitude.

Our other daughter, just twenty-three months younger, soon followed a similar course. Quite crabby one day, she was asked to go help Frannie, an elderly member of our congregation, shell peas. A grunt was her main response, but she went. Just before dinner, she burst through the back door, an ice-cream bucket half-filled with the fruit of her labor—bright green garden peas shelled and ready to enjoy.

"Here," she said, handing over the bucket. "Frannie said there'll be more in a couple of days. Can we have them for dinner tonight?"

"But I thought you didn't like peas?"

"Yeah, but these are fresh. Frannie just picked 'em. You should see her garden."

What a happy girl. Gone was the dark mood that had clouded her day. She glowed, really. She had shared work shoulder to shoulder with an eighty-five-year-old and been transformed by the experience.

Miracles come in many forms. Jesus used mud and spit. We shouldn't be surprised when those celestial blessings appear in the form of gnarled toes and buckets full of peas.

Perhaps in the course of this book you have experienced some small miracles within your family, small transformations that have brought you closer together as a family and more able to see the small miracles when they occur. Rejoice in them. Perhaps you have found more time for family by cutting back, reevaluating your strengths and weaknesses, creating routine, rescheduling your day around the "big rocks" or one of the other avenues we have suggested. If so, we rejoice with you.

But it wouldn't surprise us if in the excitement of reconnecting with your loved ones you discover something else along the way: how good it feels to serve one anther. Share the work. Make personal sacrifices for the greater good. Take time to weave those fragile threads of relationship into a strong cord that will not be broken. In the end, all that serving each other has probably made you feel a lot less lonely.

If you stop and think about it, you probably know of people (families) who were healed—in whole or in part—through serving others. "Do unto others as you would have them do unto you," the scriptures say. What the Bible doesn't specifically spell out is that doing unto others also brings healing to the doer.

Servant Therapy

Our society has always admired great servants such as Albert Schweitzer and Mother Teresa. But we need to recognize that the same spirit of service can be found in people just across the street. In our small community of three thousand, there is a retired couple that does whatever chores are needed to assist an aging neighbor couple to continue to live at home. Some teenagers in the church youth group are tired of scheduling only fun and games and insist on service projects. A single mother dropped her social life for a short time to become a catalyst—a midwife—for birthing a regional single-parent center.

In a larger city, a family of six was chosen "Family of the Year." The headline in the newspaper read: "Community Activism Is Family's Base." The list of lives this family has touched is humbling. There's a whole lot of connecting going on out there spurred on by loving actions done for the benefit of others. The funny thing is that none of these people mention the demands on their time or feeling trapped. They just talk about the love—if they talk about it at all.

Judges often assign "community service" as a consequence of vandalism or other small infractions. The person who did a wrong ends up contributing in a positive way to the very community he or she damaged. Some might call it "punishment." We call all forms of community service "servant therapy," and it's life-changing for families as well as individuals.

There are lessons to be learned and small miracles to be discovered from all this serving. For one, our sense of "us" expands. Instead of saying, "They don't have enough food to eat in North Korea; why don't we share with them?" we can actually say, "Tragically, some of us in this world don't have enough to eat even though we on this earth produce enough calories annually to feed everyone." It's not they who need food anymore; it's some of us. These seemingly small attitude adjustments move us past the confines of our own families to create larger circles—global circles that create a bond so strong that when one in the global family is hungry, we all feel it.

We are often guilty of wanting to keep our family safe and close within the family unit. When children are young, this is a good thing. But children naturally model how to expand the definition of *family*. In our case, although we still hold family vacations or time away as a priority, more often than not our kids ask to bring someone along or even to head out with their own group of friends for a little "family" time. It's a natural thing. Families never were meant to be self-serving. Our doors are meant to be open.

Isn't Servanthood
Just Another Time Trap?

How does being a servant to others fit into the theme of escaping the family time trap? Doesn't that just take more time? If we're having trouble handling everything in our lives now, won't this just add more demands and complications?

There are a number of reasons a family might try to simplify its overscheduling and reevaluate its priorities to deal with time traps. But if the reasons get stalled at "I'm doing this for me" or even "I'm doing this for us," we may succeed at changing our use of time, but our hearts remain untouched. Then it is only a matter of time before the me-me-me attitude rears its ugly head again and we return to making unhealthy choices in order to feed the ravenous appetite generated by our lusts and pride.

"It is in giving that we receive"—so goes the prayer attributed to Saint Francis of Assisi. It is in serving that we stand a chance of being healed of the very ego absorption that gets us into time traps in the first place. The word of God says, "We love because God first loved us" (1 John 4:19). It is equally true that we serve because God first served us.

At times we all need both to be served and to serve. The balance is crucial. If we act only as server, we move from being part of the family to being better than others. If we act only as the one served, we become lethargic and petty. Serving is more than just a mutual "I'll scratch your back and you scratch mine." At its core, serving really has nothing to do with us at all.

Our actions have meaning not because of what we do or what we will receive but because of who we are and whose we are. Servant therapy is family at its best. Connected to each other not by what we do or don't do, but by a simple gift of love done out of response to a God who has "destined and appointed [us] to live for the praise of his glory" (Ephesians 1:12). There's a higher calling here. May we have ears to hear it.

Make a family commitment to serve the Lord. Repent where needed. Make the necessary changes. Keep focused on the one who gave you the gift of time and the people with whom to share it. Serve where you are able. Then sit back and discover that the "trap" has been replaced by a beautiful world just waiting for small miracles to manifest themselves in buckets of peas. God bless your journey.

Connecting Points

How can we practice servant therapy in the home? You might try some of the following:

• Ask your children to agree to make each other's beds first thing in the morning.

• Serving a pet is good practice for serving other people. We asked one of our children to take over the job of feeding the dog. It's tempting to jump in and take it over again when the task gets neglected, but we found that a slightly hungry dog is a great reminder that the young person is an absolutely critical servant.

• Prepare a meal together as a family and take it over to honor a steadfast servant in your congregation.

• Invite people you admire for their service into your home. Honor and find creative ways to thank them. Your children will soak it all in.

• Write a family mission statement of one or two sentences that pinpoints what God could be doing with your family. (This is different from a family covenant. In a family covenant we make promises to our family members. A mission statement puts our faith into action.) Expand your mission statement with a mission plan. Pick an area of service that helps fulfill your family mission statement. Display your mission statement in a prominent place in your home.

* * * * *

On the next page are some suggestions for servant therapy in the church and in the home:

• Servanthood has come to the cutting edge of youth and family ministry. Make opportunities for families of all kinds to share in service projects and trips.

• Are you tired of selling candy for youth fund-raisers? Establish an account from which youth may work to draw funds for things like youth gatherings and trips. The work they do is service to the congregation and community.

• Make service opportunities available, especially for those in their late teens and early twenties, a critical time for seeking meaning in life. In Tanzania, young people are in "national service" for two years. In the United States, some choose to join the Peace Corps or church-sponsored service organizations.

• Encourage confirmation instruction in your congregation to be more than just book learning and turning in sermon outlines. Matthew 28 didn't say, "Make bookworms of all nations. . . ." It is very common for a pastor to "require" service projects only to hear what an amazing and welcome experience it was for the young, budding disciple.

• A congregation (or family, for that matter) could adopt a town with few of the advantages that your community has. We can't help every place to be healthier, but we can help one place to get medical supplies, basic health care, reading material, and so on. See if you can channel your funds and good intentions through a missionary, an agency, or someone you trust at the site. They will want to begin by meeting with community members to discern the community's needs. Participation lends dignity to all involved in the service.

• Locate and support a good service organization that is set up to make an impact elsewhere in the world. We might suggest Operation Bootstrap Africa, a Minneapolis-based

Christian organization that builds schools in several African countries.

• Ask your shut-ins to fold bulletins, do mailings, or perform other tasks, if they are able.

• Consider starting (or supporting) a mission endowment fund. Our congregation began one with a special emphasis on short-term missions. The members of our church who go out as servants of the church come back with an enthusiasm that is contagious.

Study Guide for Escaping the Family Time Trap

I n the "How to Use This Book" section of the introduction, we suggested you consider sharing the book with a small group. This study guide offers suggestions for readers wishing to include others in a four-week, small-group study of this material, as well as helpful tips for potential leaders of such a group.

Sharing a book with others that addresses important topics such as family and time can be beneficial for several reasons. Good intentions aside, it's easier to stay on task when others are running the same race. You may have worked through a problem area in your family that will allow you to offer suggestions to others struggling with similar problems. You may glean helpful information from others for your own family situations. Having various ages within the group means a wealth of life lessons available to all. And, because this is a book about families, the small-group sessions are intended for all family members, including the kids. Learning more about creating family time needs to involve them, too. Each section that follows has a similar format:

Materials Needed: supplies needed for activities

Family Time: a game or activity intended for everyone

Kid Time: specific activities for kids in grade 5 or younger (with options for kids in grade 6 and older)

Parent Time: group discussion, one-on-one time for parents or singles

Looking Ahead: planning time for putting weekly connecting points into practice

The four-week study follows the structure of this book. After the first introductory session, Parts I, II, and III will be covered in subsequent weeks. A one-night retreat or extended session is needed to complete the family covenant during the fourth session. An optional fifth-week field trip allows the group to consider enlarging its definition of *family* through a service project, as described in chapter 9.

Start-up Tips for Leaders

1. Enlarge and photocopy the cover of this book to use on promotional posters. Add the place, time, and whom to contact for more information. Pull some of the more thought-provoking quotes from the book and put them in your weekly Sunday bulletin or monthly newsletter, or tape them to the inside of the stalls in the bathrooms. A large sign by the nursery door and another at the entrance are practical places for getting the attention of busy families. Scout out two older couples whose children have left the nest to serve as mentors for the group. Reach out to the community by advertising at local day-care centers, laundromats, or grocery stores. Begin praying for the families who may be affected by this study. Sit back and see who responds.

2. Look for a young couple without children, someone who no longer has children at home, or education majors on break from college to serve as the supervisors for Kid Time. If there will be children under kindergarten age, provide nursery attendants. Good child care is essential to the program. Parents will be encouraged to participate if they know that their kids will be enjoying themselves, too. Advertise Kid

Time in your initial promotion with the names of supervisors, if possible.

3. Begin to plan the kickoff picnic or potluck. Decide if you will have snacks at the end of each weekly session and make plans for someone to handle that aspect of the planning. Consider the possibility of building a meal into the weekly program. We've had good luck at our church by offering a weekly Wednesday "Family Night" supper. Removing the burden of planning and preparing an evening meal may encourage tired parents to participate. Church members whose kids have grown might take this on as a service project for young families in their church. A free-will offering would cover the cost of food.

4. Order enough books for each family to have its own. Look ahead at the supplies needed for the upcoming weeks and set aside time to have all materials ready before the sessions start.

5. Consider keeping a scrapbook of the event or take pictures to share on a bulletin board in the church. Find someone in the group who loves to take pictures. Have new pictures from the week before available at the next class and let the kids design the bulletin board during Kid Time.

6. As the group starts to form, send out welcome notes reminding everyone of the time and place. If you are planning to begin the introductory session with food, schedule more than one hour for the session. Include on the card this quote from the introduction: "Jesus cares about families and their relationships with one another. He cares about your family, too."

7. Have music playing as people start to arrive. Consider using a theme song for the sessions. Choose something singable for all ages.

8. Take pictures of each family group as they arrive at the opening session. Include these pictures as part of a bulletin

board in your church asking for prayers as these families engage in the study.

Session 1: Creating a Right Spirit

Materials Needed

- Paper plates, cups, and so on, unless families have been instructed to bring their own. (You don't want anyone stuck in the kitchen doing dishes!)
- One ball of yarn for every fifteen people
- Supplies for Kid Time centers (explained later this section)
- Copies of *Escaping the Family Time Trap*
- Name tags, color-coded by family

Family Time

Food is always a good icebreaker and serving it is a good way to start. Be sure all participants, including children, have a name tag. If any families are present who are not church members, be sure to introduce them and welcome them.

After the meal, instruct families to form circles of fifteen or so and give one ball of yarn to each group. Begin by saying, "You're here with your family tonight and that's important. Families are important. I'm glad you've taken time to be with your family tonight/today, and I'm glad you've taken time to be with your church family, too." Keep your comments positive and short. Talk about the need for families to stay connected to each other and to God.

Have one person in the group loosely tie the yarn around his or her waist and then throw the ball of yarn to someone across the circle. That person does the same. The process continues until all people in the circle are "connected" in what looks like a giant spider web. (Note: Keep the yarn slightly loose so it doesn't tighten up on you.) To add a little competition, groups might try to walk together to retrieve a specific object, but it's fun just to do the activity for its own sake, too. Have fun getting untangled. (You may need scissors.)

With Family Time completed, send parents, youth, and children off to their appropriate activities.

Kid Time

Kids in grade six and up should be given a choice if they want to be in with the parents' discussion, work with the younger kids, or have free time. *Choice* is the big word here. Each family dynamic is a little different. Older kids who feel close to their families might benefit from a small-group discussion. Others may prefer interactions with their friends. If older children would rather just hang out while parents are in session, provide a place with videos, music, or tables for homework. Some could be put in charge of creating a "family" bulletin board with photos taken during the sessions. What's important is that participants come as a family. For some, that's a giant first step.

Kid Time activities will be formatted around four stations. Each station will remain open for the first three weeks of the study, although materials at the stations may change. For younger children, the continuity will make them feel secure and lessen any separation anxiety they may have, while the variety of the activities will keep older children interested. Introduce all stations during your opening session. Leave time for cleanup. Feel free to create your own stations or draw from the following suggestions:

Station 1: Art Center

Kids draw pictures of their families. Using fabric glue, back the picture with a piece of checkered material cut slightly larger than the drawing and glue that to a larger piece of construction paper. Tape a loop of ribbon on the back as a hanger.

Put the pictures in the hallway so the parents can admire them later.

Station 2: Story Time

Prepare a story or have a good variety of picture books and intermediate books available for kids to choose from. You might consider reading them a longer book over the course of the study.

Station 3: Building Center

Who can build the highest church steeple? Use plastic building blocks or wooden blocks. Discussion might center on where the kids live. Where does God live? Why do people make God's house so high?

Station 4: Video Theater

Many good kid-centered, Christian videos are available on the market. Choose some that encourage family connectedness. Make them available through your church library after the four sessions are over so that kids can see them again.

Optional

If one of your Kid Time supervisors is musically inclined, think about choosing a song to use during the first three weeks of the study. Kids can learn it this first session and teach it to the others during the second session.

Parent Time

As parents get settled, find three people to read the three scenarios from chapter 1. Begin the group with prayer, and introductions if needed. Pass out copies of *Escaping the Family Time Trap,* and give a brief overview from the introduction. Explain that during the hour there will be time for group discussion, conversation with spouses, and some reflection. Explain that participants will need to do some reading between sessions in order to participate effectively during the subsequent sessions.

Explain that they will be hearing three "case studies" to consider. Have the people who were chosen earlier read the scenarios from chapter 1. When they are finished, ask, "What can we learn from these stories?" (Responses may vary, but should center on the idea that everyone, no matter what their circumstances or stage in life, struggles with finding family time.) Ask participants to react to the statement by Jana from the third scenario: "We're responsible for all this [time crunch]. We created our lives just the way we wanted them." (Discussion may center on taking responsibility for the "climate" in our families and realizing that we are the only ones who can make needed changes.)

Continue by having the group break down into family units. If single parents are present, pair them together, or suggest that they write in a journal in place of discussion. Have partners talk through the three family-identity questions presented in chapter 1: Put on some soft music so participants feel free to openly share their thoughts with each other without being overheard by others.

As discussion dies down, reassemble the group and ask for responses to the question, "What are we longing for?" Write responses on easel paper or a dry-erase board and keep these statements prominent during the study.

Have participants turn to chapter 1. Read the section titled "What Do You Really Want for Your Family?" Pause between the questions to allow participants to visualize their responses. Allow space and quiet time for this. Let the quiet time evolve into a prayer for guidance as each session begins, and during the following days, to take the steps needed to bring the vision into their daily lives.

Looking Ahead

Suggest that participants go back and read the introduction and chapter 1 before beginning the survey in chapter 2. Remind them that this is a family study and point out the Connecting Points in each chapter (except chapters 2 and 5) as ways to involve children in the process. Assign the survey in chapter 2 for next week. Reassemble in the kitchen if a snack is planned. (There should be some artwork for parents to see as they pick up their kids.)

Session 2: Balancing Time and Work

Materials Needed

- New materials for Kid Time stations 1 through 4
- Time-tracking worksheet
- Jigsaw puzzle with big pieces (twenty-five or fewer pieces; each person gets one piece, so you may need more puzzles).

Family Time

When everyone is present, welcome them and introduce any newcomers. Have each person pick up a puzzle piece. (If you are using more than one puzzle, number the puzzle pieces ahead of time on the back, using one number for each puzzle.) Explain that participants are to put their puzzle together. (If you are using more than one puzzle, instruct participants to find other other participants with the same number on the back of their puzzle pieces.) When everyone is ready, set a timer for five minutes and begin. Work together to complete the puzzle. When the timer goes off, help other groups finish their puzzles. Close by saying that families are like puzzles: When all the pieces fit, you get a lovely picture or a funny moment. Everyone is needed to make the picture complete.

Send parents, youth, and children off to their appropriate activities.

Kid Time

Having established a routine during the first session, kids will move right into the four (or more) stations. You may choose to start or finish with some singing ("The Wise Man Built His House Upon the Rock" is a good one for this session) or other group activity.

The following are some activity ideas for stations 1 and 3. You may use these suggestions or come up with your own ways to tailor each station.

Station 1: Art Center

Get some clean foam trays, several large darning or plastic needles, and colorful yarn. Using a pencil, punch holes into the foam trays to spell a short word, such as *love.* Have the kids "sew" the yarn through the holes. Run a piece of yarn through the top corners to hang the work.

Station 3: Building Center

Bring together small pieces of scrap lumber, large-headed nails, and a few small hammers. Help the kids nail or glue the wood pieces together (clothespins with springs make good clamps). Some children may want to create letters or shapes with their wood and use markers to decorate their work.

Stations 2 and 4

Continue as you did the previous session. You may need to change the books and videos after the first week, depending on your group and the ages represented.

Parent Time

Ask if anybody had any good "connecting points" or family moments since the last session. Enjoy sharing success. Next, ask participants to share the areas of the survey in which they scored high (good connecting going on). Then discuss areas that seem to need attention. If parents did their homework, they should be quite ready to jump into a discussion about what they discovered.

Introduce the themes of time and work from chapters 3 and 4. Say, "We will spend a lot of time talking about time tonight. You should go home with a better understanding of how you spend your time and where you can start to budget your time in more family-orientated ways." Group participants by family or pairs (in the case of single or unaccompanied parents), and compare family schedules and reflect on the following questions:

- How much time has already been spent before you wake?

- How much free time do you actually have?

- How can you gain control of the free time in your day? What decisions might you have to make to do so?

Come back together as a large group and list examples of how participants feel robbed of time. Compare this list with the three time burglars listed in chapter 3: household chores, habitual TV watching, and overscheduling. If there is enough time, and according to individual interest, divide participants into three groups to discuss each of these time burglars. Have each group read about and discuss its chosen myth in chapter 4 and give a summary to the class as a whole. If a new myth surfaces during discussion, a group might choose to continue talking about it rather than those found in the chapter. Before closing, have participants choose one connecting point from chapters 3 and 4 to put into practice for the week.

Before leaving, draw attention to the quote you wrote on the board earlier in the evening. Acknowledge that the work/home dilemma is not a small issue for some. For those families in which both parents work, chapter 4 is an important one. Encourage them to read through it together.

Looking Ahead

Announce that chapter 5 on creating a family covenant will be covered at the family retreat or session 4. Ask participants to read chapters 6 through 8 before the next session and to try out some of the connecting points suggested. Direct them to mark or highlight sections in their books that challenged or helped them. Encourage couples to read the chapters together, out loud if possible, or to mark them in different colors if they read them separately. Their reactions to the chapters will dictate the direction of the next study.

Session 3: Creating Connectedness

Materials Needed

• New materials for Kid Time stations 1 and 3

Family Time

Reenact the children's sermon described in chapter 6. When finished, send parents, youth, and children off to their appropriate activities.

Kid Time

Station 1: Art Center

Have each child create a family banner by "stamping" his or her hands on a plain-colored piece of cotton cut and hemmed to form a table runner. Or, use burlap and fray the edges. Using the same needles and yarn from the last session, older children can sew in their family names or other words into the cloth. Younger children might trace their hands on felt, cut them out, and glue them to the cloth. Roll up the cloth and tie it with a ribbon to present to parents as a gift. Attach a small note asking parents and other siblings to add their handprints to the runner. Use the gift during family devotions.

Station 3: Building Center

Using modeling clay or homemade play-dough, have each child create a bowl to place on top of his or her family table runner. Once the bowl has dried at home, put a small votive candle in the it.

Stations 2 and 4

Continue with stories and videos from previous sessions.

Parent Time

You're going to cover a lot of ground in a short amount of time this session, so keep the discussion moving and do not let one person or group take over. Participants should already have read through the remaining chapters, but it wouldn't hurt to take the first five minutes to review the material.

With help from the participants, outline briefly some of the topics that really hit home for them as they read. (The sections in these chapters get to some of the more gritty stuff of claiming more family time. Hopefully, participants will have highlighted passages and taken notes.) Split up into small groups (couples should remain together), letting participants choose their area of interest for discussion. Once in the small groups, give them some jump-start questions or leads: "Please share one part from your essay that made you stop and think." "What connecting points hit home for you and your kids?" "What parts of the essay did you question?" "What parts surprised you?" and so on. Some groups may decide to reread their section and discuss it as something occurs to them. In either case, each group should choose one person to take notes on the discussion.

After an agreed-upon amount of time, participants come back into the large group and the recorders who took notes will share some of the highlights of their group discussions. Allow for individual responses from others if time allows.

It is hoped that all this discussion can lead to some practical decision making. Ask spouses to spend a little time talking as a couple. Ask them to come up with one concrete decision based on this material that they might do to claim more family time. They will be asked to share their decision with the whole group. It might be fun to do a follow-up during the fourth session to see how successful families have been in their endeavor.

Take time to relax and have a snack. This would be a good time, too, for children to present their banners and bowls.

Looking Ahead

You might want to think about holding a retreat (such as an overnight) for the next session, where participants will create their own family covenants. At the very least, you will need a three-hour session (a Saturday morning might work well). The process will require all family members to be present, so the kid stations will not need to be set up.

It will be helpful if one member of the family has skimmed through chapter 5, especially the "Guidelines" section, ahead of time, because all work will be done in family groups with limited leader input. Point out that families will need to bring items such as photographs, memorabilia, and Bibles. (Also see the list of materials needed for session 4.) It might be helpful to give participants a printed list.

Session 4: Creating Family Covenants (Three-Hour Retreat or One-Night Retreat)

Because a number of items are needed for this session and your budget might be limited, you might consider asking each family to supply its own materials this time. Each family will need:

- Covenant candles (one per family)
- Tagboard (see "Guidelines" in chapter 5)
- Old magazines on a variety of subjects
- Scissors and tape or glue
- Items or pictures that reflect the family's group identity as well as objects that reflect the identities of family members

Promote this aspect of the study by displaying the three phases of the covenant process: "We are . . ."; "We believe . . ."; and "We covenant. . . ." Have a large candle burning from which other family candles will be lit. Begin with a welcome and a short overview of what the session or retreat will entail. Discuss the word *covenant* and cite several places in the Bible where the word is used. Keep this discussion short. Participants will probably want to get right to it.

Walk the families through the steps for creating a family covenant outlined in chapter 5, adapting the steps to your group as needed. But remind participants that they will be doing the work with limited leader input.

If you are on an overnight retreat, it would work well to schedule one session for each step, with the first session held the first evening, the second the following morning, and the third in the afternoon. If you are working within a more compact time frame, devote at least one hour to each step. Be sure to take breaks between sessions.

Have snacks available and provide an opportunity for play or outdoor recreation. Because the sessions themselves are so structured, leave the free time free.

End with a small worship service. Bring all the covenant candles to the front to form an altar. Place the family covenants around the room to act as celebrative banners. If you've had a theme song for the study, use it to bring this session to a close. Ask individual families to take different portions of the service: readings, prayers, music. Let each person give thanks for one aspect of this shared study. Participants should respond, "We give thanks!"

Families may have prepared petitions asking God's guidance and encouragement in their desire to love each other better. Ask families to find another family who will pray for them. Family members could kneel while their supporting family lays hands on their heads and reads their petitions. Then change the roles as the first family prays for the second. Close with a group prayer of celebrative song! End with these familiar words: "Go in peace. Serve the Lord."

Looking Ahead

The group may plan to do a service project (see chapter 9). If so, make sure dates and times are announced before people head home.

Notes

Introduction

1. "Time Out," *U.S. News and World Report* (December 11, 1995): 85–86.

2. Mary Pipher, *The Shelter of Each Other: Rebuilding Our Families* (New York: Ballantine Books, 1996).

3. Albert Einstein, quoted in Dean Elias, "It's Time to Change Our Minds: An Introduction to Transformative Learning," *Revision* (Summer 1997): 2.

Chapter 2. Assess Our Connectedness

1. Dolores Curran, *Traits of a Healthy Family: 15 Traits Commonly Found in Healthy Families by Those Who Work with Them* (Minneapolis: Winston Press, 1983).

Chapter 3. Time Burglars

1. National Institute on Media and the Family.

2. Addie Jurs, *TV, Becoming Unglued: A Guide to Help Children Develop Positive TV Habits* (San Marcos, Calif.: Robert Erdmann Publishing, 1992), 60.

3. Ibid., 88.

Chapter 4. Work

1. Shannon Brownlee and Matthew Miller, "Lies Parents Tell Themselves about Why They Work," *U.S. News and World Report* (May 12, 1997): 58–64. Used by permission.

2. Ibid., 59.

3. Ibid., 60.

4. H. J. Cummins, "Paring Parents' Workweek Helps Kids, Expert Says," Minneapolis *Star Tribune* (September 5, 1999): 1A.

5. Ibid.

6. Harvey F. Egan, "At 80, He Sees That It's Not What We Do That Counts, but Who We Are—and Whose," Minneapolis *Star Tribune* (November 26, 1996): A17.

7. David Ogilvy, quoted in Brian Knowles, "Job vs. Family: Striking a Balance," *Focus on the Family* (June 1991): 3.

8. Brownlee and Miller, "Lies Parent Tell Themselves about Why They Work," 62.

9. Arlie Hoshschild, quoted in Brownlee and Miller, "Lies Parents Tell Themselves about Why They Work," 62.

10. Brian Knowles, "Job vs. Family: Striking a Balance," 3.

Chapter 6.
Determine What's Worth Our Time

1. Mary Pipher, *The Shelter of Each Other: Rebuilding Our Families* (New York: Ballantine Books, 1996), 139.

2. Barbara DeGrote Sorensen and David Sorensen, *'Tis a Gift to Be Simple: Embracing the Freedom of Living with Less* (Minneapolis: Augsburg Fortress, 1992).

3. Robert Morgan, "Life in the Blender," *Pastor's Family* (June/July 1997): 8–9.

4. Ibid.

5. Addie Jurs, *TV, Becoming Unglued*, 8.

6. James Twitchell, quoted in Jeff Davidson, *The Complete Idiot's Guide to Managing Your Time* (New York: Alpha Books, 1995), 21.

7. David Anderson, "Six Strengths of Healthy Families," *The Lutheran* (May 1997): 22.

8. Ibid.

Chapter 7. Reclaim Rituals, Make Memories, Strengthen the Connection

1. Harold Belgum, *The Twelve Days of Christmas* (Minneapolis: Augsburg Publishing House, 1974), 9.

2. Ibid.

3. Judy Ford, *Wonderful Ways to Love a Teen . . . Even When It Seems Impossible* (Berkeley: Conari Press, 1996).

4. Andrea Henkart and Journey Henkart, "Twenty-Five Ways to Say 'I Love You'" *McCall's* (August 1998): 108.

5. David Anderson, quoted in Kathryn Christianson, "Breaking Open the 'God Box,'" *The Lutheran* (May 1997): 14–15.

6. Ibid., 15.

7. Clark Cothern, "Something Wonderful This Way Comes," *Pastor's Family* (June/July 1998): 14–15.

8. Dolores Curran, *Stress and the Healthy Family: How Healthy Families Control the Ten Most Common Stresses* (Minneapolis: Winston Press, 1985), 124–125.

9. Ibid., 126.

Chapter 8. Take Time Out

1. Roland Martinson, *Effective Youth Ministry* (Minneapolis: Augsburg Publishing House, 1988), 103.

2. Susan Ashoff, "Humor: The Antidote to Stressed-Out Family Life," Minneapolis *Star Tribune* (April 6, 1998): E3.

3. Joel Goodman, quoted in Ashoff, "Humor: The Antidote to Stressed-Out Family Life," E3.